Plan to Pivot

Agile Organizational Strategy
in an Age of Complexity

PLAN
TO
PIVOT

GERRY STARSIA

NEW YORK

LONDON • NASHVILLE • MELBOURNE • VANCOUVER

Plan to Pivot

Agile Organizational Strategy in an Age of Complexity

Published in New York, New York, by Morgan James Publishing. Morgan James is a trademark of Morgan James, LLC. www.MorganJamesPublishing.com

Proudly distributed by Ingram Publisher Services.

This book was developed under the editorial direction of ASCENT, an international author coaching program, which can be contacted at info@spreadyourfire.net

A FREE ebook edition is available for you or a friend with the purchase of this print book.

```
_____
```

CLEARLY SIGN YOUR NAME ABOVE

Instructions to claim your free ebook edition:
1. Visit MorganJamesBOGO.com
2. Sign your name CLEARLY in the space above
3. Complete the form and submit a photo of this entire page
4. You or your friend can download the ebook to your preferred device

ISBN 9781631957222 paperback
ISBN 9781631957239 ebook
Library of Congress Control Number:
2021943510

Cover & Interior Design by:
Christopher Kirk
www.GFSstudio.com

Morgan James is a proud partner of Habitat for Humanity Peninsula and Greater Williamsburg. Partners in building since 2006.

Get involved today! Visit MorganJamesPublishing.com/giving-back

All net proceeds from book sales to be shared between the Margaret T. and Dominic J. Starsia Jr. Student/Athlete Scholarship Fund at the School of Education and Human Development Foundation at the University of Virginia and the Building Goodness Foundation.

TABLE OF CONTENTS

ACKNOWLEDGMENTS

The ideas in this book were developed in two very different worlds. First, based on my management experience founding and managing companies, I learned what strategic inflection points, or pivots, were and why it is important to look ahead, prepare for change, seek out opportunities, and stay alert for unplanned events. Second, for the last two decades, after a career pivot to higher education administration and the completion of my doctorate, I combined practical experience with research, writing, and teaching to be able to clarify my understanding of how and why organizations do what they do.

While teaching graduate-level Strategy and Leadership classes at the University of Virginia, my students brought fresh ideas and criticism to my own thinking, always checking my references to the underlying theories of strategy and agility and their relationship to common sense. So, thank you to my students.

Also, I appreciate those who have worked beside me, including my staff, clients, and consultants through my corporate career and my fellow administrators, faculty, and students in higher education and at UVA. To my co-teachers, Peter Brooks and Sean Jenkins, your willingness to share your experiences in my classes has been of immeasurable benefit to everyone involved. I am grateful for your collegiality, honesty, and friendship.

Turning an idea into a book is as hard as it sounds. The experience of converting an academic manuscript into useful information for practitioners is both internally challenging and rewarding. I had an idea, shortly after my dissertation was accepted, to write this book and share it, and the truth is, it would have never left my head and been transferred to paper without the coaching and advice of David Hazard. He convinced me that this work was valuable and needed to be shared. With his thoughtful and consistent urging, we plowed through the writing process together. I am forever grateful for his advice and counsel.

I especially want to thank the individuals who helped make this happen. Thanks to Alice Sullivan for introducing me to Morgan James Publishing's David Hancock and Karen Anderson. Karen's enthusiasm for my work was motivating and affirming at the exact moment that support was needed. Significant credit for the final editing, and world-class patience, goes to Sissi Haner. I am fortunate to have attracted a very professional supporting cast to get this project finished.

Last, but not least, my gratitude goes to my wife, Marianne, who did double duty while I was heads down and writing. She supported me through decades of changing priorities and careers, and when I said I was going to write this book, she encouraged and supported me. She never wavered, affirming, once again, that I am a very lucky man.

Gerry Starsia
Charlottesville, Virginia
July 2021

PART 1:

Introduction of Planning and Strategy

Chapter 1

PLAN TO WIN OR WHY BOTHER?

his past week, I spoke to three of my friends—one a college president, another an executive in a pharmaceutical company, and the other a private school headmaster—and they all had the same questions: What's going on in the world? Things are changing so fast. The climate, the economy, social justice, the pandemic. People's psychological well-being is being stretched to the breaking point, and all are seemingly moving almost faster than any of us can comprehend.

What do we do? How do these leaders, my friends, power through? How does one make decisions in such a pressure-packed, constantly changing environment? How do organizations decide what to do, prepare for change, and maintain flexibility, coherence, and focus? How can organizations create a culture where they are able to analyze the current environment within which they operate, make changes, and then pivot away from unproductive work and toward strategies that lever strengths and competencies?

Regardless of whether you manage or lead a small, medium, or large organization, these are trying times requiring really smart people working very closely together to create seamless, timely informed decisions about everything, from the work they choose to do to the work they stop doing, and the work they need to be doing, in order to be successful. This book is designed to provide some ideas and describe pathways to help traverse some of these wildly shifting conditions by sharing firsthand accounts from owners, leaders, and managers of how they comprehend their worlds and how they cope.

How I Cut My Teeth

My early career as a builder and project manager included several episodes that highlighted the frustrations of following traditional project management methods in the building of complex building projects. Over time, as I launched and operated several businesses, and managed increasingly complicated projects, I realized that the application of Agile management techniques would not only work for projects but also for my businesses. The reality is, you can't take time to carefully strategize when the very existence of your company is at stake.

My first experience with this was while at the project planning table for a multimillion-dollar construction project. The owner-developer of a shopping center in New England gave us a set of plans and wanted the project built for a certain price and on a certain timeline. After my cost estimate and draft timeline were complete, my boss and I met with the developer. When we gave him the bad news that the budget was unreachable and the timeline unrealistic, he blew up, threatened to cancel the contract, and walked out of the meeting. So, we decided to go back to the drawing board and create a set of options or scenarios for the next meeting that consisted of a set of reachable scopes of work and timelines—and let the developer pick his own path forward. We suggested that "if you give us the leeway to move ahead with pre-agreed upon options, and if the conditions are favorable to move ahead with some, we will do so." By taking the initiative and return to the drawing board, we created a rolling list of options for the project, built trust with the developer that we were working in his best interest, built into the project a number of options that had been put on hold, and in the end delivered a win-win for both sides.

Later, in a career move to higher education financial and operations—which included the executive management of these large, slow-moving organizations—the frustrations of following traditional strategic planning and management techniques pushed me toward what had worked well in the past: using an Agile approach to management.

While "Agile" has been traditionally related to software development and more recently to innovation teams, my career path provided the opportunity and situations to apply the Agile approach to construction project management and, later, to the strategic management of higher education institutions. I have utilized Agile techniques as a project manager, project executive, owner representative, and later as a chief operating officer at two top business schools in the US. In the latter role, I was a doctoral student studying the application of complexity theory in strategic planning processes. In that research, I found a connection between Agile, complexity, and strategy—essentially, a new model for strategic planning and strategic management. My perspective is broad and deep, beginning as a practitioner and, most recently, as a scholar. I've been on boards of directors for both for-profit and nonprofit companies and organizations and have provided executive advisement to a number of CEOs. This book provides a baseline understanding of the research, the practices, and the stories and lessons learned. What you read here can help you apply these ideas and those circulating in the "Agile management" literature to your own practices and management challenges. Now, let me show you where my personal and professional insights come from.

What I Learned, Coming from the Ground Up

After an unsatisfactory experience at a college in New England, I returned home without a degree. I wandered my way through several jobs, including as a partner in a small contracting company, a carpenter, and a plant engineer. Having no industry experience or contacts in commercial construction and needing some stability and focus in my professional life, I applied for a job as an estimator at a large commercial contracting company in New

York City. I was always good with numbers, and the job as a cost estimator seemed to be a good place to start. Most of the projects were in New York City and the surrounding area, and I really enjoyed deconstructing complicated projects, analyzing the various components, and then putting together detailed estimates that were the basis for bids and proposals. Once the contracts were signed, I worked with the project managers to purchase the subcontracts and materials and then supported them in the field as needed. Frankly, I took to project management like a fly to honey and, in short order, was promoted to project manager and then project executive, managing the project managers. Most of the projects were in high-rise commercial buildings; they were complicated and difficult to manage; untangling the complications and overseeing the work required technical expertise, long hours, and quite a bit of moxie. Along with the satisfaction of driving these projects to completion, there was also plenty of frustration.

There were times when the contracts between general contractor, subcontractors, and consultants never seemed to work correctly, and the relationships typically soured. In other cases, no matter what happened, things went just fine. In these two examples, what was different? In business and project management, managers rely upon a cadre of subcontractors and suppliers to perform their segment of work at a quality, cost, and timeline that is provided by the developer/owner/contractor and consistent with what is expected overall—and all have their own agendas and incentives. Subcontractors often know more about their individual area than the contractor (e.g., software programmers and trades like electrical, plumbing, and HVAC). They know where and how to cut corners that are, in many cases, contrary to the interests of the owner-developer. The cat and mouse games between the general contractor and subcontractors are extremely frustrating and expensive, often resulting in disagreements and lawsuits—a result that is in no one's best interests—wasting time, money, and psychic energy. On the flip side, there have been times when subcontractors were cooperative, supportive of the project's goals, and performed superbly. What a relief!

Where are your business or organizational frustrations coming from right now? Have you pinpointed the sources yet? Gotten to the root cause of issues? If you haven't taken a careful look, I highly recommend you do.

I also experienced firsthand the frustration of planning, which, in this case, was part of the preparation for managing complicated building projects. Trying to make sense of someone else's vision for a project through the lens of a set of one-dimensional plans and specifications, often created by designers and architects with little to no field experience, was difficult. It required patience and careful analysis fraught with significant risk. It required being able to visualize what the designers intended and then interpreting that vision and communicating it to the tradesman tasked to do the actual work. This complicated cognitive process of interpretation and communication of someone else's vision is at the core of how the design and building industry operates, a process that is underappreciated and often results in disputes and disagreements. Managing this is a critical part of the project manager's job and often results in many projects coming in late and over budget. It is this process that needed to improve. Over time I began to apply many of the principles of what has become known as an Agile framework in some large, complex construction projects, initially in my own design-build business and later as a business school chief operating officer.

After years of estimating and managing low bid, low expectation projects where the customer and the contractor often found themselves in adversarial positions, I knew there had to be a better way. So, in the mid-1980s, I launched a design-build company specializing in laboratories, medical facilities, and hospital projects. We were focused on complicated medical and laboratory projects and took a "turnkey approach" to the work. Architects, engineers, and project managers—working as a team—would work with the customer to plan the project based on their vision, create a budget, refine the plans, and get the project built. The core principles of the company included: 1) building our expertise in managing complicated medical projects and 2) designing projects in-house in order to control the scope of work, the cost, and the timeline. This unique approach to managing projects by partnering with our customers in a "one-stop-shop" was a very early example of applying Agile principles to construction-related project management.

When I started my company, I wondered if it was possible to stick to my values of honesty, integrity, and quality and still be successful. Would my customers appreciate and value that approach? If so, could this be the foundation of and differentiator for my company in an industry with a reputation for dishonesty, conflict, and project failure? If so, what is my vision for the company? How can I estimate the likelihood of success, and what might that look like? How do I plan? How do I manage?

I learned that knowing and living your core principles is a very good thing. They need to be at the heart of all you do. They must guide your decisions, even in changing, challenging situations. Over the course of my early project management career, it became evident that low-bid, high-risk, high-stress project management was not a smart, long-term business strategy. Certainly, another approach was needed. It made no sense to spend significant amounts of time and money pursuing owners, developers, and investors in an effort to build their projects, only to not meet expectations, struggle with subcontractors and suppliers and wind up with all parties unhappy. There simply had to be a better way. It was at this point that the company began using Agile principles to manage projects long before Agile was cool.

We Were Agile before Agile Was Cool

We initially began using Agile techniques to manage change orders: the change of scope, costs, and timeline that inevitably happen on every project. A reoccurring pain point for everyone involved, change orders happen—in some cases, due to an error by the architect, and in others, due to a request by the owner for additional work ("while you're at it, add this and that…"). But, regardless of cause, change orders add complications, distract the subcontractors and suppliers, and add tension to the relationships between the general contractor and the architect, the general contractor and the subcon-tractors, and the general contractor and the customer. As a result, to better manage this change process, I began assembling Agile teams long before the term Agile was in vogue.

How did this work? What we did was keep one team, our base contract team, laser-focused on building the base contract project, and when change orders came up, we would assign them to a separate change team (using Agile techniques) to design, budget, and then thread the new scope and costs into the baseline work. This required the customer, architects, engineers, and our Agile change team to work closely together to manage changes in a way that caused a minimal amount of cost additions and delays. The transparency required to follow this process kept all stakeholders keenly aware of any changes and the project delivery implications. Everyone felt the pain, and everyone worked together to minimize the aftereffects. Did it work perfectly? No. Was it an improvement over the traditional approach? Yes, with the company's reputation growing and improving based on this new customer-centered approach. We didn't call this "Agile" then, but we all knew it was cool.

The Strategy Scholar Who Despised Strategic Planning

After a successful and stressful almost-decade-and-a-half in the design-build business, my wife and I made a lifestyle change and relocated to Charlottesville, Virginia, a small college town in the mid-Atlantic. While originally planning to buy some real estate and build projects, I accepted a job as the chief operating officer at the McIntire School of Commerce, a top-ranked, primarily undergraduate business school. When I arrived, the dean and I talked about his priorities, which included the renovation of an existing 1960's era building, imagined as a new facility that was more indicative of a world-class business school, with all the modern amenities required to attract world-class faculty and students. Before we get too far into the story, let me offer some context related to planning and the higher education industry. The first thing you should know is that until Peterson,

Dill, Mets & Associates (1997) and John Bryson (2017) wrote their higher education planning texts, the most recognizable book in the higher education arena was *Academic Strategy* by George Keller, published in 1983. Planning was simply never standard operating procedure for most colleges and universities, and those with strong brands and reputations, and certainly most faculty, ignored the idea. In general, academics and higher education administrators thought: Why bother planning when students were beating down the door to be admitted?

If you were to measure success for an undergraduate business school, my new employer certainly checked (and still checks) a lot of boxes. The dean, a well-respected strategy scholar, transformed a business school that had been focused on accounting degrees into one emphasizing finance, including hedge funds, private equity, and consulting—career paths that were much more lucrative and donation-friendly. During his long tenure as its leader, the school became a global powerhouse perennially ranked in the top two or three in the world and was, by most measures, successful and stable. In this case, the planning-related story is twofold: 1) The school had no strategic plan, and 2) because we had business and capital savvy alumni-donors, we needed a responsive and participative plan for our new building project and as a result, applied Agile techniques to oversee and manage the work. This story was also about the strategy scholar-dean who hated strategic planning and yet appreciated a new, fast-track approach to design and building the new facility that saved both time and money.

When I first arrived at this new job, I completed an assessment of the business model and financial health and noted that the undergraduate degree program, where all expenses were allocated, was underwater; the tuition revenue didn't cover expenses. As the flagship program of the school, this situation forced a decision: Do we lower our aspirations, reduce costs, and balance the operating budget, or do we find other new sources of revenue? Fortunately, the school had a strong reputation in the business school world, and along with the institution's brand, had several very good options. Starting with partnering with one of the top five accounting firms for a custom MS in Accounting Programs that guaranteed a minimum number of seats at market rate tuition, cash flow increased, and we had some financial breathing room.

It was obvious we needed a more comprehensive plan in order to identify additional new sources of revenue, decide which new programs to launch, communicate the dean's vision to the rest of the organization, and avoid the stress and strain of negative operating results, but for the time being, the wolf was not at our front door. How could we be successful and meet our aspirational goals without a strategic plan? When I approached the dean with this question, he said he wasn't interested in a strategic planning exercise and frankly preferred to wing it—and that's what we did: We held the undergraduate enrollment flat and focused on growing the graduate program. If you measure success by rankings and alumni sentiment, then the school was a success, but what's not in that measure are the missed opportunities and increased impact that were possible had we taken a more strategic and deliberate approach to our work.

In a recent conversation with a staff member, it was confirmed that immediately upon being appointed, the new dean assembled a strategic planning task force that, among other priorities, proposed three areas of focus: 1) diversity, 2) expanding admissions, and 3) new programs to reach more students.

For example, in terms of numbers and composition, the school's undergraduate enrollment is the same in 2020 as it was in 2000, so a lot of students missed out on, and continue to miss out on, the terrific faculty and programs offered. Issues, including a lack of student and faculty diversity, persist as the school continues to admit students based solely on grades and test scores. By remaining inwardly focused, protective, and static, the school missed opportunities to share the faculty's unique teaching and academic expertise with a broader, more diverse audience.

Interestingly, in 2020, a new dean was hired, and in a number of conversations with staff, she has taken a different approach by organizing planning teams that include students, faculty, and alumni in order to broaden participation and input. They are beginning to make strategic decisions as a team, and while the school has brought professional staff into the planning process, the dean has indicated her interest in building a sustainable, informed, and focused organization capable of addressing the challenges of operating in the hypercompetitive environment of elite business schools while also offering programs to more students of diverse backgrounds, thus having a much greater impact in the world.

In addition to stabilizing the revenue base with steady, predictable enrollment and programs and steadily moving up in the rankings, we also raised the money to build a new business school building, and in early 2012, I was appointed building committee chairman for the renovation of a historic building, a project that when complete, would cost over $71 million and take thirty-eight months to build. Originally planned to cost $65 million and take thirty-six months to build, the project was substantially completed within two months of the planned completion date with a final cost of construction 8% or so above the original estimate. By all measures, for a project of this size and complexity—and when considering the myriad state regulations and other uncontrollable institutional overhead added to the budget—the project was a huge success. How did that happen? Well, we followed an Agile project management approach that had never been tried before at this university.

What We Were Up Against

For any of us who have experienced the bidding process for contracts with the state or federal governments for anything from paper towels to jet planes, we know these relationships can be complicated, adversarial, and often unsuccessful for all parties involved. Typical state construction projects have historically been low-bid affairs highlighted by runaway costs and missed deadlines, leading to subpar design and building quality. Go to any public college campus in the US, and you will easily be able to pick out the state-funded buildings from the privately funded ones—and our campus was no different. The Library and Student Commons buildings, funded with state money, looked nothing like the Business and Law School buildings, funded with private donations.

This was the first project to be attempted at this institution on a fast-track, cost-plus basis. Since it was fully funded with private donations, the institution's leadership allowed the project to proceed without a fixed price. The project team, including the customer (in this case, the business school and the university), the architects and engineers, and the construction management company, worked together to develop a baseline budget and schedule. As the business school defined their programmatic needs, guided by the architects and engineers, schematic plans were budgeted by the construction manager and reviewed by all.

This was the first step in a continual cycle of "draw, estimate, and adjust" that kept the project team focused on the customer: to build a facility that met the needs of the school (scope of work) while staying on budget (money) and on schedule (time). This process, what I refer to as "early Agile," followed this collaborative set of steps until the plans were finalized and approved for construction. Once the design was set and agreed upon, construction got underway with the project management team moving out of design and into implementation or project management that included, among other tasks, the management of design changes and change orders. The budget and timeline were adjusted each time the scope changed, either by a field condition (e.g., subsurface rock or water where it wasn't supposed to be), design mistake (e.g., a calculation error), or the customer's request (e.g., we want another ten rooms of classroom storage cabinets).

In order to stay on schedule and manage changes using the Agile approach, a separate Agile team(s) handled the design and budgeting of the changes, minimizing costs and timeline extensions. As construction activity ramped up and changes occurred, either by the customer's choice ("we need more electrical outlets") or as a result of field conditions ("we didn't know there was rock under the ground where the foundations belong"), the price and schedule were adjusted. If there were additional costs and timeline extensions, the customer had the option of reducing costs elsewhere or approving the added cost and time to the project. By maintaining the finish date of thirty-six months as a priority, as the inevitable changes came up, separate Agile teams were formed to focus on changes and decide on scope, best value, and when and how to move forward. Once the team agreed, the additional work was dovetailed into the base timeline.

As a result, while the Agile team handled the changes, the base team continued to work on driving the baseline schedule with changes either brought into the baseline work or completed on overtime—all with the goal of maintaining the timeline. The project team had the authority to make decisions, everyone's voice was heard, and the school, responsible for paying the bill, made the final decisions. In the final analysis, the project had an original timeline of thirty-six months and was delivered in thirty-eight; it had an original construction budget of $41 million, was delivered for $44 million, and delivered the quality and level of finishes imagined at the start. By all accounts, the project was a tremendous success.

Without the parties working together, this project would have certainly cost more money and taken more time. This "fast-track" or Agile approach was new to capital project management and considered very innovative. In fact, it has become the project delivery method of choice for the institution. Once again, we were using Agile for higher education facility projects long before the term Agile was applied to these kinds of building projects and long before it was cool.

Back to operations. In another example, when I assumed the job of a chief operating officer at another school at the university, there was no strategic plan to rely on for program direction and decision-making. Instead, understanding the school's priorities and areas of focus would require a series of meetings with the executive team and faculty who led the research institutes and degree and executive programs. Resistant to formal strategic planning, the executive team decided where to place "small bets" to fund pilot programs that were of interest but hadn't yet been tested. For these ad hoc strategic initiatives, we organized what could best be described as Agile teams of experts charged with creating one- or two-page plans, including a scope of the project, budget, timeline, and performance measures (e.g., How many students? How much revenue? How much expense? How will the program be marketed?). These plans were reviewed every six to eight weeks to check on the progress and decide whether to increase our investment and commitment for promising projects or reduce or cut off funding. While this approach served as a useful model for short-term decision-making, without a strategic plan, these continuous pilots had the potential to cause strategy drifting and shifting without direction or focus—with no one, other than the executive team, knowing where the school was headed.

"Management is neither a science nor a profession.
It's a practice. And the practice fundamentally doesn't change.
What changes is the content of what you're dealing with."
—Henry Mintzberg

In my experience, using an Agile approach has been useful and outperforms other more linear and traditional options, whether there is an urgent need to identify an approach for your construction company or project or you are managing an organization. In the business school examples, ad hoc Agile processes were followed rather than formal strategic plans. Individual proposals were pushed up to the executive team by faculty leaders or suggested by executive team members, without cadence or strategic justification. The proposals were reviewed by asking questions like: "How does this project support the school's strategic mission? What is the timeline? How will funds flow into and out of the project? What non-funding resources are needed?" and then by matching short-term proposals to what the executive team thought was viable. While this resulted in the team being hyper-focused on the implications of any new strategies, it is difficult to know how much potential was missed (e.g., financial support, new programs, increased enrollments, etc.). As was learned by the next dean, a former executive and strategy expert from a major consulting company, this lack of formal strategic planning held the school back from achieving its full potential and created lots of opportunities for growth and expansion.

A Management Pivot

Using Agile to create dynamic, rolling plans that require review and adjustment every three months or so works well as a strategic planning framework. In this world of hypercompetition, globalization, and communications, it is becoming increasingly difficult to plan much more than three to six months into the future. As a strategic management framework, Agile's principles of putting the customer's needs first, creating more value from less work, decreasing complexity by reducing large projects into smaller parts managed by small teams, constantly scanning the environment for opportunities and threats, and bringing smart partners into the process has created a revolutionary way of doing business. Successfully used by companies like Microsoft, Spotify, and SRI, companies able to mesh operational expertise, opportunities uncovered during the planning process, and technical expertise will win the day. So, design a one- to three-year plan that will serve as a vision of the future, communicate your vision, and utilize an Agile approach to manage the strategy implementation process. This is the end-to-end process that will drive competitive advantage and sustainable positive results.

Lessons Learned:
1. Without a strategic plan, institutions and organizations, even perennially successful ones, can lose their way and miss opportunities.
2. Without accountability, leaders can avoid creating strategic plans derived from internal and external assessments and agreed upon by the organization's stakeholders.

3. Planning, like filling out annual reports, meeting with direct reports and key employees for annual reviews and grinding your way through the day-to-day management of any organization is hard work and, if allowed to be avoidable, is avoided.

4. Formerly referred to as "fast-track," a new approach to managing projects is the application of Agile software principles to design and construction.

5. As learned by the McIntire School building project team, once a project gets underway, using Agile teams to manage changes—and the integration of those changes into the baseline scope and schedule—minimizes the cost and schedule impact.

6. By applying Agile principles to managing the operation, McIntire was able to place "small bets" or pilot programs as a way to test new ideas before making major changes.

Chapter 2

A COMPLEX SET OF CONDITIONS TO NAVIGATE

When we prepare to travel, many of us set an itinerary, purchase tickets, check the Weather Channel for local conditions and pack the appropriate gear. Similarly, leaders of twenty-first-century organizations of all types—large and small, profit and non-profit, local, regional, national and international—need to prepare in order to take the controls of even the most modest enterprises. A research study by the author, "Strategic Planning in Higher Education: An Examination of Variation in Strategic Planning Practices and Their Effect on Success in NCAA Division I Athletics" (Starsia 2010), examined how planning is necessary to complete basic tasks like taking a trip and how the process of planning can also have a profound effect on the success of organizations.

In the study, he found that four variables were correlated with the success of university athletics departments: 1) the competency of staff, 2) scanning the environment for threats and opportunities, 3) avoiding a top-down approach, and 4) making frequent changes to a plan. All are directly correlated to success, generalizable to many other industries, and all are discussed in more detail in the research study. This book is an extension of that research. It describes important new approaches to strategic planning that every organization should consider, how planning—when seamlessly connected to implementation and strategic management—creates a powerful new way to manage organizations, and then describes the implications for success. While the study is discussed in detail later in this book, the highlights include:

1. The traditional strategic planning frameworks, models, and instructions found in how-to-plan handbooks available in your favorite bookstore and touted by consultants are no longer of much value and,

2. Certain characteristics of planning, including staff competency/ level of training, systematic and constant scanning of the external environment, top-down organizational structures, and the frequency of plan changes, were found to correlate with the success measures.

Why does this matter? And what does it have to do with planning? The findings from the study indicate that while none of the three planning models designed by the author were correlated with success, certain variables or planning characteristics were. These results provide a more refined and nuanced way to plan *and* indicate that a new complex planning model is emerging, one that combines the unique characteristics identified in the study, along with others commonly associated with complexity theory.

While some critics say planning is out of date and no longer relevant, I disagree and suggest that when these characteristics are combined into a new planning approach—one that I call Agile Planning—it offers organizations a way to create a valuable plan that, when combined with other Agile principles, results in a continuous approach to managing that provides both a vision of the future and a dynamic way to manage the day-to-day operations.

In the early days of my design-build business, it was a terrific example of NOT applying Agile principles to management. When I started, I managed this multimillion-dollar enterprise on a single spreadsheet that listed the projects, along with basic information (e.g., project owners, contact information, estimated value, time to close the contract, and probability of closing the contract), and projected cash flow and profit and loss. Kept in a file on my desktop computer, no one else had access to this information, and I didn't discuss the project and financial projections with anyone in any detail. Of course, this wasn't helpful to those in charge of marketing and sales. Nor was the lack of forecasting helpful to the estimators trying to balance the portfolio or the project managers trying to plan for staffing and other resources—but that's how it worked at the time, with some success. Over time, it became evident that this homegrown way of doing business was unsustainable and what followed was the development of sophisticated software capable of tracking marketing efforts and forecasting sales, along with integrated cost estimation and project management delivery targets—all layered together in a single, integrated, and increasingly powerful business intelligence system. With the separate functions of estimation, project management, and finance manually managed and the integrated reports manually assembled, this early version of a business intelligence platform brought instant information, group work sharing, feedback, and analysis to the prospecting, contracting, and financial management processes. As these systems became increasingly automated and less expensive, they were available to businesses of all sizes. As an early adopter of the power and value of business intelligence (BI), our company's data grew to be more current, directional, and accurate as we scaled the business.

The world is changing. In a single lifetime, many of those reading this book will have owned their first cars manufactured by quintessential mid-twentieth-century names like Ford, Chrysler, and General Motors, and more recently purchased cars from companies with names like Toyota and Hyundai, and all-electric vehicles from companies like Tesla, Rivian, and NIO. Imagine the differences between these groups of vehicles. The early to mid-twentieth-century vehicles looked similar, spewed emissions, and were unreliable; mid-late twentieth-century vehicles were the classic "muscle cars," heavy steel frames and bodies and big gas engines, the "boardwalk cruiser"; and most recently, the all-electric vehicle with no emissions, fewer parts, and exceptional reliability. Mechanically, the earlier vehicles were simple machines consisting of an engine, transmission, braking system, and steering wheel—sitting in a heavy steel chassis and finished off with a cool paint job. When these cars needed repairs, you took them to the mechanic down the street who was able to source the parts, make the needed fix, and you were back on the road quickly and inexpensively.

Let's compare that experience to the typical owners of the early twenty-first-century all-electric vehicles, using Tesla as an example. Often described as "rolling computers that happen to have wheels," these vehicles are mechanically simple, with one or more electric motors, a battery pack storage system, and an electronic control system. In a recent interview, Elon Musk, Tesla's CEO, described the vehicle as a highly sophisticated computer system or "platform" and suggested that over the lifetime of a Tesla, the owner will be able to upgrade the functionality of the vehicle through virtual software updates. By creating a simple mechanical vehicle controlled by a programmable software "platform," these cars are capable of longer life and unlimited, on-the-fly upgrades and improvements. No need to buy a whole new "platform," just keep the motors running and occasionally upgrade the software. When a Tesla needs service, it requires the trained skills of a Tesla engineer or mechanic familiar with the complex and proprietary computers that drive the system. These vehicles, and many similar, modern brands, require taking the vehicle back to the dealer. Mechanics are trading in their Snap-On socket wrench sets for a computer diagnostics station or, better yet, spending time at Tesla's system engineer training school. The evolution of the modern vehicle, as seen through the lens of these two vehicles, is nothing short of extraordinary, and amazingly, it all happened over the course of a single lifetime. As you will see, the story of the evolution of planning and management follows much the same path.

How the Book Is Organized

At the book's conclusion, I will propose new techniques that, when applied to strategic planning and management, will make the process more efficient, applicable, and valuable. These new ideas will help leaders and managers of all types of organizations navigate in this era of hypercompetition and dynamically changing internal and external conditions. It's a brave new world out there, and this book will help you understand it and manage it.

As a leader in business education, with connections throughout the global business community, I can tell you that, across the board, leaders are experiencing stress and frustration in the area of business planning. They are being pushed by boards and stockholders at one end and pulled at the other end with calls for help from rank-and-file managers and employees in the organizations they're expected to lead. Like many of your peers, you may be asking:

- Why bother planning (and spending the time and money to do so) if the final product is largely ignored?
- How can my organization apply the insights and ideas developed as a result of the planning process, help drive decisions, and guide strategic direction?
- Will this approach to planning improve my organization's performance and lead to greater success?

First, I will address these questions by applying my research findings and over four decades of personal experience—and the experiences of other business and organizational leaders—to current organizational and leadership challenges. I will then explore the process of strategy making by describing the process of plan creation and the transition from plan creation to implementation, and then will explore how a plan's implementation affects commonly used strategic management techniques. Next, you will learn about the critical nature of the transition stage, which—similar to passing the baton in a relay race—can be relatively simple but also extremely important to the success or failure of the plan. And finally, we'll share ideas related to those instances where organizations quickly shift direction—what I call "PIVOTS."

I'll also address questions such as: Once the planning is over and the baton has been passed, how do managers manage? How does the new model help managers make decisions?

Familiar one-dimensional planning processes that consume hundreds of staff hours and take months to complete need to be replaced with more dynamic processes that include customers and staff and are tied to uncovering opportunities and leveraging competencies. Hierarchal, structured organizations with top-down strategies need to be replaced with robust, multi-dimensional sets of action steps and collaborations, resulting in greater levels of sustainable organizational success. To build these action steps, those tasked with planning need to consider how certain characteristics of complexity theory should be applied to the planning process and decision-making. This new planning approach is not a set of prescribed tasks with a structured and predictable result but rather a continuous process that adapts to ever-changing competitive threats and opportunities—it is less a planning exercise and more an approach to strategic management. Planners, leaders, and managers alike will find the proposed theories and suggested processes both informative and critical to setting out an organization's mission, vision, values, and goals—the keys to developing a strategy.

> *"Everybody has a plan until they get punched in the mouth."*
> —Mike Tyson

When I read about the decision by the California state higher education system to suspend all face-to-face classes and the dining and living facilities for the 2020 fall semester in response to the pandemic, it occurred to me that this decision, while bold, flies in the face of many other institutions that are planning to maintain operations "as close to normal as possible." Most institutions agree they will minimally require facemasks for the fall semester and encourage students to social distance. Many are either unable or unwilling to make further, more significant changes, yet others are holding in-person classes. How is it possible that so many institutions in the same industry can come to such different conclusions after researching and evaluating the same situation and talking to peers and experts? This living and unfolding case study amplifies both the difficulties related to strategic decision-making and the inherent and inconsistent ways organizations implement their strategies. It's not for the faint of heart!

You may also be asking: If we're in a rapidly changing world and business environment, why bother planning at all? According to the research, organizations that plan outperform those that do not. However, for any activity to be deemed worthwhile, it must deliver benefits to the organization. It is not acceptable to create a plan that is largely ignored, never to be revisited, until the next siren calls for a new plan. When done well, planning requires a significant expenditure of resources. Strategic plans are the foundations upon which strategic management and Agile management are built. The objective should be to make planning and Agile approaches the operating framework for your organization, highlighted by continuous adaptation to current conditions and action, or listen to a few opinions and take your chances.

It seems to me that we live in an age of planning as fast as our synapses can process. For nonprofits attempting to share their message and build philanthropic support, they are finding an increasingly competitive industry crowded with well-run organizations pursuing the same group of donors. For small businesses, trying to capture market share from other more experienced and stable companies makes the identification of customers, and the pursuit of new business, a survival strategy. For large businesses, there is constant competitive pressure to grow by extending existing product lines into markets that are most likely to increase profits and keep the shareholders happy. Where are these new markets? What do consumers want? Who are the likely competitors? How will we exploit the opportunities?

Radical Adaptability

The rapid pace of change is disrupting organizations of all types and sizes, in all industries, and increasingly interrupting our lives. Advancing computer speed, ubiquitous communications, and artificial intelligence are all creating a convergence of humanness and machines and work and leisure. Throw in "black swan" events, such as a global pandemic, deforestation, and sea-level rise, and the result is unplanned and profound societal and organizational disruption that pushes companies and institutions to rethink how they fundamentally operate.

How are some organizations adapting? In the case of Unilever, the consumer products conglomerate, they were pressed by their customers during the pandemic to Pivot from their regular line of products to hand sanitizer and went from idea to market in six to seven weeks. In the case of Craig Slingluff Jr., a University of Virginia physician who had been leading a team of cancer researchers for over a decade, he was asked to apply his experience on a melanoma vaccine to COVID. His team made what he described as a "quick pivot" from cancer to a vaccine, insisting this was not a distraction but rather that "each project informs the other" (Gard 2020).

Described as "radical adaptability," these two examples of Agile management demonstrate that, among other lessons, organizations benefitted from their teams' ability to achieve better collaboration, more accountability, creativity, and growth; and in the case of UVA, had the infrastructure and experience to seamlessly and successfully Pivot from their core product to an alternative (Ferrazzi 2020). In the Unilever case, they were guided by a "go-forward plan" that followed five Agile steps to deliver value fast:

1. Priorities are based on what is most important to their customers.
2. Teams should prepare detailed briefs on each project that is shared and discussed.
3. Get to work. De-emphasize process and deliver value, fast.
4. Pilot, experiment, test, and demo early work with a broad group of stakeholders.

5. Learn fast, complete retrospectives, share lessons learned, and move forward.

Variations on the above five-step process are peppered throughout this book and are meant as information for you, the reader, to use as you construct your own Agile approach to managing your organization.

Building Back Better

In a recent *Forbes* magazine article titled "What Does It Mean to Build Back Better?" Sarah Kaplan, a professor at the University of Toronto's Rotman School of Management, said that "Build Back Better" is an expression coined by a UN Task Force charged with coming up with improved disaster-recovery plans. For them, building back better meant using recovery after calamities—they were thinking of earthquakes, tsunamis, and hurricanes—to restore equitable social systems, revitalize livelihoods, and protect the environment. Don't just rebuild houses—install clean water systems. Don't just improve early warning systems—create safer roads and dwellings (Kaplan 2020).

As it happens, this book was written during the COVID-19 pandemic, which forced individuals and organizations to adapt rapidly to new, dynamic conditions. In this context, build back better means making good on the commitments to stakeholders beyond financial gain and share price appreciation. Steve Denning suggests that the pandemic will have vast biological, economic, leadership, political, social, and moral implications for years, if not decades, to come… resulting in new ways to work, new ways to learn, new ways to lead, and new ways to live (Denning 2020).

What lessons are organizations learning that are likely to stick post-pandemic? What we can be sure of is that business as usual is off the table. Companies of all sorts are learning how to work from home, communicate with customers on Zoom, and deliver value to customers with little to no social interaction at all. Some are moving forward rapidly with digitizing platforms and workflow, using Zoom and other sharing technologies as substitutes for in-person work, resulting in less need for office space and less travel and travel-related costs. In addition to Denning's "mechanics of adapting" as described above, the crisis has also created opportunities for companies such as Netflix, Amazon, and S.C. Johnson; all have enjoyed increased business and valuations.

In contrast, firms along the hospitality spectrum (e.g., hotels, airlines, casinos, cruise lines) have taken significant hits to their bottom lines. Learning how to adapt will make some organizations stronger, some weaker, and some disappear. Regardless of industry, organizations need to learn to adapt and develop Agile practices, fast.

One industry not known for its agility is higher education. During the 2020 COVID pandemic, in the spring semester, institutions had to Pivot from face-to-face instruction to online in a matter of a few weeks and then, facing unprecedented uncertainty, plan for the fall and spring semesters. As institutions began to announce their plans, a survey of more than 350 college presidents and provosts conducted by *The Chronicle* revealed that a plurality opted for face-to-face instruction, though many also pursued hybrid in-person/online models as contingencies, preparing to Pivot to online if forced to do so. The watchword in this extreme uncertainty seems to be flexibility (Gardner 2020).

Employees need safe and flexible working environments, virtual communication tools, and to the extent possible, stability—all qualities attributed to Agile management. While Sarah Kaplan described how post-COVID organizational focus must be directed toward sustainability, she also points to the need for Agile organizations. She said, "Companies will need to transform how they operate in ways that we are only beginning to imagine" (Kaplan 2020). In a different article that repeated this theme, Soren Kaplan, consultant and affiliate faculty at the USC Marshall School of Business, suggests there's a quiet revolution going on in corporate America that is about being lean, focused, and maniacally strategic (Kaplan 2012).

Crises, like sudden unexpected opportunities, provide the situations and urgency to think more deeply about how work is done now for both start-ups and big companies and highlight the need for flexibility and strategic agility in the future. Steve Denning suggested that the COVID crisis, for instance, served as the "Great Accelerator" to both explore new ways of learning, leading, and living and to test the limits of civil rights and the consolidation of power at the expense of democracy (Denning 2020b). As a result, society as a whole had to accelerate its examination of all these important ways of operating, with Agile increasingly relied upon as the management approach of choice.

Turning a Battleship

While Agile management techniques are more easily adopted in smaller companies and organizations, rapid transformation is much more difficult for larger entities. Yet, despite the challenges, some are working at it:

1. Intuit uses daily "lean-in start-up" across the company to match teams with rapid experimentation experts.
2. Kimberley Clark is prompting one-day "expert acceleration sessions" that connect external thought leaders to business teams to keep the ideas fresh and focused on breakthroughs.
3. Whirlpool is using a network of mentors loaded with innovative tools to help teams focus on market change.

Apparently, you *can* teach an old dog new tricks! Soren Kaplan suggests there are a number of strategies that firms can use to jumpstart innovation, many of which are Agile and asymmetric and innovative, including 1) follow your customers, 2) tap into outside collaborators, 3) stay small and nimble, and 4) use the best of readily available products and tools and then invent whatever is needed to combine the new and newly developed into a breakthrough product (Kaplan 2012).

Two questions: 1) What would organizations have done had they known in advance that the COVID pandemic was coming? And 2) what should organizations do in anticipation of the next unplanned event? The answer is: Get Agile, "maniacally" and "relentlessly."

Preferably, of course, we won't wait for an epidemic or other disaster to move our organizations away from slow-moving approaches to managing and toward Agile principles. Leaders need to stay alert to the relentless shifting of context in the form of competition, globalization, and technological advances occurring every day. The increasing speed of change means we need to abandon the old way of doing business and find, test, and develop new operating models.

Let's step into some creative thinking here. Imagine you are the CEO of an executive search firm whose reputation includes timeliness, in-person recruiting, and high levels of customer service. With a burgeoning industry in online resumé curation and using information technology techniques to connect with companies, the need for in-person interviews and a "personal touch" are becoming a thing of the past. The competition looks more like a technology company than a recruiter using online tools and videoconferencing to get work done. What do you do?

Or let's say you are a name partner in a law firm in New York City, with Park Avenue offices and plenty of associates providing legal services to financial services, manufacturers, and service firms all over the world. In the past, when your clients in the EU or Asia called, a partner would jump on a jet and show up the next day in the client's office. They really appreciated the service, but recently, they have complained that the firm's billing rates, and overall costs, are increasing unreasonably fast. The clients are telling you they can find lawyers on the internet capable of turning around advice and documents in a twenty-four-hour period for a fraction of the cost. What do you do?

How about this scenario? You are the president of a state college with a reputation for training and graduating K-12 teachers. Located in western Pennsylvania in an area best known for mining and steel production, the population is decreasing, and young people are moving away from the region, headed for cities in the east and south. Highly reliant on state support and tuition, enrollments have dropped by over 35% over the last five years, and state support has been flat. What do you do?

The Days of Simply Planning and Measuring Progress Are Over

*"The days of 'plan, execute, measure, and adjust' are over.
In the twenty-first century, creating a vision, meeting with
customers, defining their goals, then assembling smart teams,
distributing work, and iteratively responding to the
customer's market experiences is where it's at."*
—Anonymous

In all the preceding examples, they demonstrate dramatic and rapid shifts away from more traditional ways of operating toward new Agile approaches. In the search firm example, that CEO needs to move away from a twentieth-century, office-based consultancy business model and develop a network of recruiters who link their individual work to a core platform that warehouses information and resources and distributes and manages leads. This virtual community would be able to minimize travel and overhead activities and related expenses by developing leading-edge technological solutions for the recruitment, interviewing, and hiring processes, and while some face-to-face meetings would still be needed, there would be fewer, resulting in an accelerated process with significantly lower costs.

In the law firm example, the firm could build a global network of legal specialists who are able to connect to the network and support clients virtually at a fraction of the cost. In the higher education example, the president needs to develop certificate and degree programs based on the needs of regional companies that recruit the graduates, develop new sources of revenue (e.g., philanthropy and executive programs), and build alliances and partnerships with employers to place students in internships and jobs. Interestingly, in the search firm and law firm examples, these service-provider organizations have moved to a distributed model with the partners managing clients remotely and the firm adding little value, other than name recognition.

So, what role does "the firm" have in these new virtual networks? While that is still to be determined, the reality is that this new way of work is already happening today all over the world. The way firms do business in almost every industry has fundamentally changed, particularly after the pandemic took hold.

Some experts say that planning is dead, and spending time planning in this rapid and dynamic business environment is a waste of resources. Since 2010, I've been researching and writing about whether the time and money spent on planning is worth it. I am more convinced than ever that planning is an investment, a critical element in successful organizations, and the key for organizations to stay focused and relevant and successful.

Regardless of the organization type—whether profit or nonprofit, service or professional—many people ask planning experts: "How do I begin a strategic plan?" and "What does a good plan look like?" The response most often provided is to look on the web or find a good book on planning and follow the guidelines. But therein lies the first problem. Since there are plenty of resources available to use as a framework, it may not be obvious which ones best suit your organization. Very quickly, too, you run into a second problem.

Planning Is Neither Simple nor Easy

The truth is that planning is hard. It is contextual and multi-dimensional. While firms of all types may manage similarly once the planning is done, they first need to tailor their plans to fit their strengths, opportunities, size, structure, competitive environment, and aspirations. Small firms don't plan in the same way as larger ones. New firms, busy making markets and establishing their place in an industry, plan differently than those who have been around awhile, and technology firms plan differently than manufacturers. Planning is also organizational and conditions-specific. Some firms have an abundance of professional staff (e.g., financial, technology, legal, etc.) while others have more labor-intensive expertise (e.g., manufacturing, logistics, construction, etc.), and some firms are necessarily local and regional while others are national and global. In short, "one size does *not* fit all."

Where does that leave you as a leader who needs to plan for the future vitality and success of your organization? How do you plan when the conditions in which you operate continually change? Having been in your shoes as the founder and president of a number of companies, later as a consultant working with a number of for-profit and nonprofit firms, and most recently leading three schools at a major university, it is obvious to me that 1) planning is valuable, 2) those included in the planning process need to be carefully chosen and should represent important segments of the organization, and 3) how plans are developed and communicated *is a valuable process* and critical to your organization's success.

Planning Is Hard Work

The biggest barrier: Planning is hard work, and many leaders, when able to avoid the process, don't want the responsibility or accountability that planning creates. I have worked with bosses who sigh and complain about the process. In many cases, staff and other stakeholders ask questions related to a program or project that is strategic in nature and could be/should be easily communicated in a simple plan but is not. In my experience in higher education, deans often brushed off strategic planning as "a waste of time" and "unnecessary," and then the school's board of directors and the institution had no idea of the direction and, importantly, their role in moving the organization forward. Simply stated, no one at the institutional level held these leaders accountable. As a result, none of the schools realized their potential. Opportunities were squandered, and board members and others lost faith in the administration's ability to manage successfully, and as we will see in other cases, this phenomenon is certainly not limited to higher education.

Planning Also Isn't Sexy

Planning is one of those activities that just isn't sexy. For leaders whose descriptions in the leadership literature run the gamut from Transformational to Adaptive and Authentic, many leaders prefer to give speeches, meet with customers, and promote the organization—without doing the hard work of planning and managing. They are often too busy being "the symbolic leader" than leading. Similar to the NFL player who enjoys the recognition that comes with the two hours of football on sixteen Sundays in the fall, it's important to remember that in order for them to enjoy the limelight of Sunday afternoons, they've had to spend their lives training and preparing for these infrequent and relatively short bursts of fame. Similar to the efforts of the typical NFL player, if leaders don't spend the time to learn their craft by using tools like strategic planning and Agile management frameworks and approaches, developing teams of motivated experts, and systematically scanning and analyzing the competitive and industry environments, they run the risk of not making it to the "big game."

Planning is the Organization's Connective Tissue

The fact is, planning in the constantly changing environment in which every leader must operate is actually an ongoing *process* and keeps their organizations healthy and growing. In an earlier version of strategic management, and in several companies and later schools I worked for and boards that I joined, these organizations set up annual meetings to consider their strategies and revise their strategic plans. Many of them were struggling, and none purposefully connected the planning and the managing. Strategy is a process that begins with planning, followed by piloting projects, and then selecting which will survive and which will go. Those are the basic steps in creating and managing strategy. The people involved in the process continually assess the environment and adjust the plan and performance. Results are analyzed and possibilities considered. The communication of the strategies across functions, up and down the structure, and inside and outside the organization becomes the connective tissue that binds intention to action.

This book describes a new, adaptive way of thinking/viewing/reading signs and various portents and opportunities. This new way of "seeing the playing field" needs to be baked into the culture as a core value and core competency. It must be second nature to everyone at the executive table, starting with the board and the CEO, and then passed along to the VPs, managers, and staff. Everyone needs to know what the organization stands for, what their customers need, what they will do, and how their individual efforts contribute to success. Unfortunately, in almost every corporation and organization I've worked for or been connected to, this has rarely been the case. For many of the case studies, planning was a drag, no one enjoyed it, and the overwhelming sentiment was that the sooner it's over, the better. What a colossal waste of time and money and, thus, the reason for writing this book!

As a recent example of how this works, let me share a personal story. My father was a patient at a local hospital. A teaching hospital and regional tertiary care center, the facility has hundreds of beds and is busy, with many of the very best doctors in the world. It has also been described as cold and impersonal, and when I visited him, I asked about the services he was receiving. He told me that while the doctors and nurses were terrific and he felt he was in good hands, he really interacted with this one staff person who gave him a shave and brought him a few things to make him comfortable. He spoke about him for most of the visit, and it occurred to me that this is how the patient, in this case, my father, experiences the hospital. It's not the marketing campaign or slogans that matter. It is how the patient (or customer) "feels" at the point of service. The lesson: The organization's reputation is often earned in the field, at the point of service, and not in the executive offices. So, listen to your customers, invest in your people, and embed the core values and strategies priorities within every person in your organization. That's the recipe for success.

There is No "How-To" Guide

This book is not intended to be a how-to guide to strategic planning. What it offers are tools you need to design a process that's tailored for your organization and seamlessly connects to management. It includes an overview of the strategic planning process, along with a collection of processes and models you can rely on as your own planning process gets underway.

"Plans are useless, but planning is indispensable."
—Dwight Eisenhower

I want to tell you upfront: When planning is useful and effective, the process becomes more like *a way to operate* rather than as a prescription to follow. It is much more like the trail map for a long hike or the navigation charts for a sailing adventure—and *it will change* according to weather, traffic, and conditions. The challenge is to prepare the organization for the inevitable changes ahead and the Pivot *that follows*. The leader or driver or captain has to stay alert and make continuous adjustments, and in some cases, investments, in order to stay on course and reach the destination. In the chapters that follow, I describe the process of planning, describe how pivoting works, and share frameworks for change.

Why Planning, and Why Now?

We live in complex times with a lot of "unknown unknowns," and the challenge for organizations is to manage this state of unknowingness. This book proposes a way for organizations of all types to cope with that state of affairs, beginning with how they decide to do what they do—that is, how they plan. Of course, no two plans are alike, and rarely do CEOs, board members, or leaders approach planning or value the process in the same way. In case study examples detailed later in the book, you will learn about the context and the real-world planning stories. You'll see through the eyes of colleagues with whom I've worked, including the dean of a highly ranked business school and world-class strategy scholar, the dean of an education school, a seasoned engineer and nonprofit board member, and a well-respected hospital CEO—all struggling with the strategic planning and implementation processes. These stories provide context, along with first-person accounts of how executives from different industries considered planning and management, and in many cases, chose reactive and ad hoc approaches to deliberate and systematic ones. So, what's going on? Like Occam's Razor, perhaps the simplest principles at work are the most likely to be true: In strategy and planning, one size doesn't fit all, context matters, and as an often-undervalued process that costs money and takes time, planning is often largely avoided and ignored. For those organizations that ignore the benefits of strategic planning and Agile implementation, as you will see, they do so at their own peril.

Strategic planning and strategic management processes have never been more important than they are today. In fact, John Bryson, a well-known strategy scholar, dedicated a chapter to it in his latest book, *Strategic Planning for Public and Nonprofit Organizations*. The chapter, "Why Strategic Planning Is More Important than Ever," drives home the point that the speed and scale of change underway, on many dimensions, requires organizations to "think, act, and learn strategically as never before" (Bryson 2018, p. 7). As we move into the third decade of the twenty-first century, every organization needs to make time to consider where they are positioned within their competitive set, where the opportunities exist in the markets, what kinds of products and services they are able to offer at high value and low cost to their customers, and the future direction of the organization. At *minimum*, organizations need to design a plan and share it internally in order to share a common vision with employees, and it should include the performance goals that its leaders are responsible for delivering. Strategy must become part of an organization's culture if it is to survive and thrive in the face of rapid change.

It is when planning, strategy, and culture meet, and Agile principles added, that the secret sauce of successful strategic *planning* and strategic *implementation* result.

What's in This for You?

Change now comes at every one of us at lightning speed. New technologies spring up and make obsolete technologies we rely on… and which we invested in just eighteen months ago. Virtual meetings; battery-powered cars, trucks, and aircraft; artificial intelligence-powered consumer product platforms; robotics; and on and on—in one or two decades, and certainly one lifetime, the world has profoundly changed. And that is why, in this book, I will extend existing strategic-planning theory into a newly emerging area of study that takes these conditions into account—chaos or complexity theories. These studies have at their core the idea that organizations are networks that evolve and expand, developing patterns of behavior or action much like biological systems (e.g., snowflakes or seashores or honeybee colonies).

In fact, organizations that survive and thrive act less like machines and more like organic communities. To help you apply these new ideas and ways of managing, I'll offer a framework that takes all of these factors into account.

In short, I'll help you recognize the ways in which our rapidly changing world and work environment affects planning, requiring that an Agile approach to managing organizations is adopted and implemented. I've included an outline of new aspects of planning, along with detailed descriptions, that will prove useful for organizations of all sizes and in all industries—a "one-stop-shop" for those of you beginning the planning process and wondering what to do and how to do it.

Chapter 3

WHAT IS STRATEGIC PLANNING REALLY ABOUT?

I f the environment is changing so rapidly, how can organizations plan for the future? What is a reasonable time horizon for organizations to consider when planning? How often should the plan be re-visited and reformulated? Before we dive into these questions, let me define some terms and explain a few fundamentals related to *strategy*.

Strategy is a pattern of actions and resource allocations designed to achieve an organization's goals. *Strategic management* is the implementation of the organization's goals and strategies, with both activities being driven from a *strategic planning* process (Bateman and Snell 2002). Recognizing that there is a transition between the strategic planning and strategic management processes, it is safe to say that managers need to master the tools and techniques related to strategic management, including the ability to rapidly transition from the static environment of planning and creating structure to the ever-shifting world of markets, competition, and changing priorities.

This book is about how to create a meaningful strategic plan, how to apply its goals and values, and then how to move from plan to action and back again. It's targeted at anyone thinking about the future of their organizations—regardless of industry size or type; whether for-profit or non-profit; multinational, regional, or local; large, mid-size, or small—and is useful for those responsible for choosing the direction of their organizations and/or leading a strategic planning program, at the very least, as a tool to brainstorm ideas.

Some of you have studied management in business school, and others have learned it on the fly. The temptation is always to skip the basics, believing you understand what strategic planning and management mean or skipping over them because you fear you don't, and that's uncomfortable. There is also the myth that once a colleague ascends to a leadership position, they automatically become smarter and more strategic, which in practice has been proven to be a bunch of nonsense. Let's take a quick look at exactly what experts are talking about and why understanding the purpose for and execution of planning should be important to you.

What Are Experts Talking about Specifically?

Experts in the field of business studies define *strategic planning* and *strategic management* as follows:

- *Strategic planning* is a disciplined effort to produce fundamental decisions and actions that shape and guide what an organization is, what it does, and why it does it (Bryson 2004). It may also be defined as the process of developing and maintaining a strategic fit between the organization and changing market opportunities (Bateman and Snell 2002; Kotler and Murphy 1981).
- *Strategic management* is a systematic analysis of an organization's internal and external environments, the purpose of which is to leverage its strengths in the implementation of activities that support its purpose.

In both strategic planning and strategic management realms, the terms "disciplined effort," "process," and "systematic" are used despite that, in practice, there is very little about management that can be described as such. Why does this dissonance exist, and what does it mean to managers? Simply stated, the world is speeding up and becoming increasingly complex, so managers need to learn to move faster and react quickly to opportunities and threats. How do we manage hyper speed and complexity? Consider recent research and case studies for ideas related to moving forward.

Look to Nature to Comprehend Organizational Complexity

When executed at the rapid pace necessary to be effective, planning, like management, resembles natural systems (e.g., beehives and forests) much more so than the linear, step-by-step processes of the past. In his book *Business at the Speed of Thought*, Bill Gates (2009) describes the integration of business and technology tasks as a "Digital Nervous System." He alludes to a connection between the technological dimensions of organizations, assumed to be housed within the information technology infrastructure, and the activities of its inhabitants, assumed to mimic a biological system. He uses the nervous system metaphor to describe how, in organizations, information is always flowing, and corporate stimuli are instantaneous and critical to its functioning. The concept that information and biological systems are related, at least metaphorically, can also be applied when considering left- and right-side brain function with the left side housing the systems, or literal dimensions of idea generation, and the right side the intuitive or conceptual. This relationship between information flow and biological systems—the left and right sides of the brain, systems and conceptual thinkers, task managers and strategists, planners and doers—is at the very heart of this book. Systems thinkers believe that if all variation can be identified and quantified, then outcomes become predictable. Intuitive thinkers know that it is virtually impossible to track all variation and that by using a complexity-theory-based view of information flow, the best way to make sense of this vast collection of data is by identifying patterns and managing outliers. *When operating seamlessly and in concert, planning and management are more like a fully integrated continual process than a series of individual decisions and actions.* How this integration works and how to manage it is the subject of the chapters ahead.

So, What Does This Have to Do with Planning?

Despite the instantaneous and rapid-fire nature of the environments in which we work and live, CEOs, presidents, leaders, managers, and consultants have to look to the future and plan ahead *in some way.* In fact, planning is not only as relevant as it has always been, it is even more imperative in a post-Great Recession and post-pandemic world. It is true that, due to the explosion of information and the ubiquitous nature of technology, the very nature of planning has changed—recently and rapidly. Still, many believe they can "wing it" or "make it up as we go along." So, allow me to walk you through my decades of experience and careful examination of organizational planning and what I've learned about the critical need for a next-generation planning and management process.

Now that we've checked the "planning" box, let's do what we were going to do anyway.

My interest in strategic planning began a number of years ago while working toward my doctorate. As the resident higher education strategy expert, two professional colleagues asked me for advice with these questions: "How do I find information on strategic planning, and how do I get started?" and "We just completed a strategic planning process that no one pays attention to. Now that we've spent all this time and money, the plan will sit on a shelf and gather dust—so why should we bother?" It occurred to me that the long, arduous process these people had gone through had indeed been a tremendous waste of time, and I wondered: Why do smart people spend time doing this work if it yields nothing positive for the organization—particularly when resources are so hard to come by?

It also occurred to me that organizations can no longer afford to invest in these kinds of activities when it is challenging enough for everyone involved in an organization to keep their heads above water. If a plan is important, why do so many people ignore it, ignore taking the time to consider the future, and ignore the benefits of having a clear windshield through which to see the organization's actions and avoid the potholes and swales along the side of the road? Is the avoidance of planning a people or process problem? Here are a few stories that may shed some light on these questions.

From my years in the corporate and higher education worlds, I knew the planning process sapped time, energy, and money, with the resulting plan largely ignored. An absolute waste of time and energy. In a world of constrained resources, I knew none of these organizations had neither the time nor money to waste and had heard too many complaints that "We did all this for nothing."

Curious as to why such a dynamic might be at work, I made a decade-long journey through the strategy, management, and strategic planning literature, wrote a dissertation, and read every book and academic journal article related to strategic planning. A common theme that emerged was that a number of the widely accepted models and frameworks seemed to be out of step with the challenges being faced by twenty-first-century organizations, and the literature and research had not kept up with the conditions on the ground. The situation was changing fast, and planners and leaders were using twentieth-century approaches to manage.

In a *Wall Street Journal* article titled "Strategic Plans Lose Favor," the writer described companies as needing to "shift their course on the fly," confirming what I had suspected: Strategic planning was undergoing a period of significant and profound change (January 25, 2010, p. B7). The opportunity costs were too high to hesitate when making decisions. As a result, companies needed to develop new ways to develop their plans and prepare for changes along the way. It became obvious that the creation *of a culture of strategy-making*—highlighted by the development of adaptive, multi-scenario rolling strategies in lieu of rigid, five-year plans—was needed. In case you're feeling slightly resistant (I can hear some of you thinking, "Who has the time for this? I'm already working hard to keep up."), let me explain why planning as a guide to managing complexity matters by sharing a few personal experiences.

Planning Helped My Company Punch above Its Weight Class

As the founder of a medical design-build company in the mid-1980s, I needed to figure out how to grow the company by identifying areas of expertise that were different or unique, how much demand there was for these services, and how to scale the company. It became apparent that if we were going to be a run-of-the-mill construction management company, we would battle with a large number of competitors who were better financed with deep customer relationships—an advantage that would be difficult to overcome. In a stroke of brilliance or luck, we decided to focus on medical clients and developed deep expertise in very complicated medical imaging and radiation therapy projects. We differentiated ourselves, minimized most of the competition, and were able to demand premium prices—all in a commodity industry. After we launched the company and enjoyed some early success, we needed to stabilize the operation, so we completed a strategic planning process that included staff, customers, suppliers, and business owners, laying the groundwork for over a decade of profitability.

Beer and Insight

After exchanging warm greetings and personal updates during a recent round of happy hour drinks with a few colleagues working in senior positions at the university, the subject quickly turned to university business. No surprise there as our institution was in turmoil. As the beer flowed and the volume increased, the big issue of the day surfaced: the recent change in leadership at our university. After a period of unusually stable institutional leadership that included a twenty-year presidential term, a COO who had been in place for over thirty years, and a two-term provost, all of whom were graduates of our university, the university hired a new president, executive vice president and COO, and an executive vice president and provost—the top three positions—and none held degrees from our school. Obviously, significant change was on the horizon and, of course, we knew what needed to be done! We argued about reorganization, personnel changes, the economic environment, state and federal funding for higher education, the rising cost of tuition, and the role of intercollegiate athletics within the institution. Finally, one of my colleagues asked: "How can we move forward without a strategic plan?"

Wasted Potential and Planning Missteps

I smiled to myself. In the early 2000s, as the newly hired COO of a top-ranked undergraduate business school, my new boss said: "we don't have a plan" and "don't need a plan" in response to a request to see the school's strategic plan. It was (and still is) breathtaking that a top-ranked business school, led by a world-class strategy scholar, had no strategic plan, and counter to what was happening in the rest of the business school industry, with new degree programs, executive education, corporate partnerships, and certificates being quickly added to elite school portfolios, the dean insisted the school remain small, launching only one new program over my twelve plus year tenure. It certainly was a story of missed opportunities, and one could only wonder what more could have been done if the executive team, board members, faculty, students, and alumni had been included in a strategic planning process.

Suggestions to extend its world-class programs around the world, share the amazing knowledge and expertise of the faculty, and improve its focus on diversity goals were largely ignored. As a result, the classroom experience wasn't as rich as it could have been, and for those of us in senior positions, we began to realize that the students coming through our programs came to reflect these narrow values. So, while we were proud of our top national rankings and perennial market dominance, these were truly missed opportunities.

I moved from the undergraduate business school, accepting the Sr. Associate Dean and COO position at the graduate business school. In this new assignment, while there was extensive strategic planning documentation available to me for review, unfortunately, the plan was out of date, incomplete, and not well communicated. The school's executive team, each of whom was responsible for individual functional areas (e.g., degree programs, executive education, the faculty, student affairs, and operations), had no goals, no timelines, and no real accountability, making performance measurement nearly impossible. In my last year in this role, in preparation for leadership succession, I teamed up with the outgoing dean to run an extensive, strategic planning process that included faculty, staff, students, alumni, board members, and institutional representatives. The dean wrote a case study focused on the school and its current state (e.g., SWOT and competitive analyses), followed by an extensive strategic planning session that discussed the future. A consultant led a discussion that included alumni, board members, faculty, and staff to better understand the MBA market, what skills employers were looking for, and how program design and industry needs could be more complementary and closely aligned. The program's strengths and weaknesses were listed on the whiteboard, along with significant competitive threats, and at the end of the session, opportunities were identified, along with an agreement on the priorities for the upcoming year or two. Through this cooperative process, stakeholders determined potential paths forward for the school, participants became familiar with one another, and trust was built. At the session's conclusion, a clear strategy document was produced that served as the basis for a now shared and public plan, with the participants energized and requesting that the process be repeated at the end of next year. A win-win for everyone involved and a great example of the *process* being valuable, not just the plan. This process and the final plan would prove extremely valuable to the new incoming dean.

Most recently, as the executive director and chief fundraising officer at the education school, it became immediately clear that the school's leadership had no experience with, nor any interest in, planning. During the onboarding process, when I asked about their plan, the dean said there was no strategic plan available. When I pressed him on this topic, he said, "We've spent two years in a strategic planning process, the faculty are exhausted, and I'm not interested in doing any more planning." As a result, while the dean often referred to "the plan," each department (and each faculty member) operated on their own with very little collaboration or cooperation. Lots of talk and no action. Lots of potential, no progress. As a result, over the course of the next two to three years, without stated priorities and strategic initiatives, fundraising sputtered, and important academic projects foundered. In short order, it became apparent that fundraising would never be successful unless the fundraisers could link individual and corporate philanthropy to the school's strategic priorities. And while the school's fundraising performance eventually improved largely due to additional investments in staff, performance plateaued, and many opportunities were missed.

On a More Local Level

In another example, I was a member of the Board of Directors for a small, local nonprofit specializing in the design and construction of critically needed schools, clinics, homes, and community centers. This organization builds structures and trains workers to help people rebuild their lives and their communities. Over the past year or so, the organization has undergone significant change. After more than a decade of carrying the organization on their backs, the founders were burned out and needed to recruit new board members. These new members brought fresh perspectives that included ideas related to the growth and management of the organization. Recently, the focus of the board meetings had centered on expansion. Did it stay small and enjoy our success or should they expand and build more goodness in new regions? Could it replicate the specialness about the organization that both protected its core vision and allowed them to respond to crises regardless of where they occurred?

The board members were split on this expansion question, with some wanting to remain local and others wanting to grow with the latter group, saying, "Why not spread more goodness!" During these deliberations, something happened that changed everything, at least for a while—a major earthquake struck Haiti. Despite a history of managing projects locally and regionally, the crisis in Haiti was viewed by a majority of the board as just the kind of project that would benefit from this group's expertise. Rebuilding teams were immediately organized to travel there and identify potential Haitian partners and projects. Despite having completed a number of projects that helped a significant number of families, building goodness in this part of the world stressed the organization's staff and financial resources. It became obvious to the board that a decision about the organization's strategy and direction was ahead. The extensive media attention that followed the Haitian rebuilding projects generated sizable new donations. The board debated what projects would be in the portfolio and which would be denied. Should the focus be on local, regional, national, or international projects, and if so, how did that affect the organization's structure and strategy? We talked about the portfolio of projects, the project mix, and the difficulty of being "all things to all people." In the end, we agreed that we needed to "focus." One of the members said, "If we want to sort this out, we need a strategic plan."

Why am I sharing this story? Unfortunately, the business landscape is strewn with epic failures, including Xerox, Kodak, and Blockbuster, and while strategic planning is neither the antidote to poor management nor the answer to every organizational ill, what it can be is useful when organizations need to focus their work, target certain kinds of projects or products, reassess what they are doing, and prepare for the future. What was said in the boardrooms of these corporate failures is anyone's guess, but it is likely, for whatever reason, that these leaders lost sight of evolving conditions in their industry and the importance of continuous innovation. How did Kodak miss the move toward digital photography? How did Xerox miss the move toward digital printing? How did Blockbuster miss the move toward streaming video? In all these well-documented corporate failures, many people lost jobs, and multibillions of dollars of value evaporated in the blink of an eye. If these former industry-leading companies, with all the resources and expertise they accumulated, can fail, so can you. If an elite institution can miss opportunities and squander potential due to a lack of accountability and little to no focus, so can you. In the following chapters, you will see what needs to be done to get your organization on track and stay there.

How Should We Plan?

When I began my research into strategic planning, I was absolutely convinced that good plans make successful organizations. In fact, I found that much of the research, at least prior to 2005, supported this thinking (Armstrong 2005; Mintzberg, Ahlstrand, and Lampel 1998; Porter 2000). This last decade is different, however, and the paradigms of the past are no longer valid. More recently, new strategy-related research is focused on the adaptation of complexity theory to strategic planning and management, and considering the world as it is today and how approaches to planning are affected, we need to ask some important questions.

For current managers and planners, one simple principle should drive this work: Customers are the primary focus of all that companies do. In the past, manufacturers and service providers offered products they believed filled a need or niche, often as a result of market research and often with little to no input from customers—a "build it and they will come" strategy. In the twenty-first century, organizations have to live by the "customer is king (or queen)" philosophy or risk missing rapidly evolving markets. In addition to this simple mantra, managers also need to rely on tools and techniques borrowed from Agile project management theory to prepare for adjustment as markets and demand shift over time. The contemporary Agile organization requires smart, well-trained, and highly aware staff able to apply technical expertise to analyze markets and deploy competitive strategies. Simply stated: Every member of the organization, along with their customers, is needed to help determine, communicate, and disseminate plans and drive strategy.

Plans Are Not Prescriptions

What I can say with certainty is that strategic plans are *not* prescriptions, remedies, road maps, or blueprints—so don't even bother starting a plan if this is your goal. I can also say that leaders need to develop skills and aptitudes in order to see patterns in their organizations, nimbly adjust to changing conditions, and then move forward. If you want to successfully plan and add value to your organization, you will need to learn a new way to think, act, communicate and, ultimately, make decisions. You will need to surround yourself with smart, open-minded thinkers capable of participating in deep conversations that result in next-generation strategic ideas. And you will need to pilot new ideas, evaluate their performance, and support them or discontinue them quickly and objectively. This continuous process, which is not an activity that starts and finishes with dates certain, needs to become embedded within the culture of your organization. Ignore this and risk losing your competitive advantage. Pay attention to the recommendations that follow and risk success.

Ideas Grounded in Research and Experience

This book is grounded in research and based on leading-edge theory, case studies, and first-person examples. In the case studies, readers can peer inside the strategic planning processes of six organizations in healthcare, higher education, nonprofit, and an industry association, all of different sizes and levels of complexity, with the goal of identifying those aspects of planning that may be common to all and those that may be unique and situational. The founders and the board members of the small, closely-held foundation experience stress related to different visions of the future that bogs down the strategic planning process and overwhelms decision-making; the large hospital follows a strategic planning process dictated by the umbrella corporation, which is largely impractical and adds little value;

the university whose two different presidents delivered planning processes that were very different in substance and effect; and finally, the strategic planning process of a successful and stable industry association. You will be able to compare firsthand how these very different organizations plan, communicate their plans, and how their planning process affects their strategy and performance.

In the research project that inspired this book, I focused on higher education athletics departments and attempted to build three planning models with the goal of understanding how each, or any, of the models correlated with organizational performance as measured by financial performance, graduation rates, and championships. While the intention of the study presumed that one of the models would be more strongly correlated to any or all of the success factors, after the data were run and analyzed, none of the models in and of themselves were more or less correlated to the success factors. Rather, the data showed that certain individual characteristics found in *each* of the models were. Those characteristics, when combined, are the basis for a newly emergent Agile management theory that is just beginning to take hold in recent writing and scholarship. Two other important findings from the research project were 1) the decentralization of strategy creation correlates to success and 2) strategic planning should be part of a strategic management culture where planning and management come together. What follows is a quick example of what I mean.

Some industries traditionally considered to be slow-moving and bureaucratic, like the military, have brought planning and management together following Agile principles. For example, General Stanley McChrystal, the leader in charge of military operations in the Middle East and Afghanistan, learned that traditional military might consisting of heavy weapons and munitions (e.g., aircraft, ships, and large numbers of soldiers) was ineffective when faced with an extremely mobile and under-resourced enemy encountered in that region. The general realized he needed to adjust and adapt his planning and execution in order to fight this enemy in that part of the world and quickly changed his strategy from a linear approach to a very complex one. That kind of adaptation is at the heart of organizational agility—that is, the ability to Pivot, to shift and change directions based on environment, industry conditions, and competition.

Military leaders, CEOs, and college presidents will need to develop the skills necessary to continuously process change and make adjustments, often on the fly, in real time. Like the NFL quarterback who changes the play at the line of scrimmage, or the multilevel chess game between Captain Kirk and Dr. Spock on *Star Trek*, or the chess master in the Netflix movie *The Queen's Gambit*, these leaders will need to visualize multiple moves ahead. They need to see the playing field as it sits now and well into the future.

Changed Perspective

My current research on this subject, beginning as a business owner in the 1990s and as a scholar and teacher in the 2000s, has shifted my own perspective from planning as a structured activity to being part of an approach or a process, and—maybe most important of all—*a way of thinking*. For organizations and their leaders, *being consciously Agile* is a way of thinking that is increasingly looked to as the dominant way to plan and execute and adjust and plan again. If my perspective can change, so can yours. In the next chapter, we will look at how planning and strategy, when blended into a continuous process, provide organizations with the best chance for success.

Chapter 4

WHAT IS STRATEGY, AND HOW DOES IT WORK?

"There are two kinds of puzzles; pat puzzles and puzzling puzzles.
Puzzling puzzles are about creating new rules to get around old,
broken ones requiring solutions that are outrageous,
until they turn out to be obvious."
—Henry Mintzberg

While sometimes seeming to be, as Mintzberg suggests, a puzzling puzzle, management is nonetheless a way of interpreting an organization's abilities and matching them with the needs of customers and consumers. As explained to my advisees and coaching clients preparing to either enter the workforce or looking to advance, the simple truth is that managers who are looking to off-load projects often drop them onto the desks of new employees. How do you manage this? Where do you start? How will you lead? Well, you need to have a working knowledge in two areas, project management and strategy, before you get started. Assuming you have project management experience and/or training or know where to get it, let's focus on how to understand and develop strategies.

A strategy is a pattern or plan that integrates an organization's goals, policies, and collective actions into a cohesive whole designed to ensure that basic objectives are achieved (Hax and Majluf 1984). A well-conceived strategy will inventory an organization's resources and allocate them according to its long-term goals, aspirations, market position, and environment. Ironically, many organizations have difficulty developing a shared vision around missions, goals, strategies, and budgets and are "most likely to succeed when and where they are least needed and least likely to succeed when and where they are most needed" (Bryson and Finn 1995, p. 249). Mintzberg, Quinn, and Voyer (1995) say there are four basic dimensions of strategy:

1. Goal identification, policymaking, and action sequences to achieve those goals;
2. Development of a few key thrusts around which resources are placed and actions taken;
3. The building of core strength of purpose in such a way as to resist the forces of external distraction and competition; and
4. Designing a supportive hierarchy and organizational structure in support of the above.

Strategies range from more deliberate forms, including planned, entrepreneurial, and ideological, to mostly emergent forms, including process, disconnected, consensus, and imposed, to very emergent, including iterative and chaos. Strategic planning is a process that determines an organization's mission, vision, values, and goals; sets overall organizational objectives; determines the basic approaches to be used in pursuing those objectives; and then determines the means to be used in obtaining the resources to achieve the objectives (Drucker 1988).

Mintzberg organized the different approaches to strategy as "schools of thought," each with a distinct approach, contributions, and limitations. Take a look at the table below from "Mintzberg's Schools of Strategic Thought."

SCHOOL	PROCESS	APPROACH	CONTRIBUTIONS	LIMITATIONS
Design	Conception	Clear strategies formulated in a deliberate approach	Order and architecture	Overly simplistic
Planning	Formality	Rigorous set of steps followed leading to a strategy	Clear direction and control	Top down. Consensus too easily attained.
Positioning	Analytical	Using industry context, how to improve position	Increased scientific approach	Ignores political, environmental and other externalities
Entrepreneurial	Visionary	Relies on the leader's wisdom and experience	CEO clarity can provide vision	Over-reliance on one person
Cognitive	Mental	Analyzes participants and activity patterns	Strategy is cognitive, creative and emergent	Strong conceptual but not practical
Learning	Emergent	Lessons learned lead to a plan of action	Begins to deal with complexity and ambiguity	Bias to "learn" with little to no "doing"
Power	Negotiation	Strategy developed between holders of power and stakeholders	The strong survive. Issues are debated. Consensus is achieved.	Can be divisive and political with little to no strategy resulting
Cultural	Collective	Strategy is a collective and cooperative process	Social processes, beliefs and values have a role	Can be divisive and political with little to no strategy resulting
Environmental	Reactive	Response to external environment	Environmental focus	Vague and supportive of status quo
Configuration	Transformation	Able to move from one decision-making structure to another	Strategy is closely pegged to original design	There are many original forms, not just those defined by the leader

The strategic plan is the output resulting from the strategic planning process. While it would be terrific if it were simply the development of a written plan, there are, in fact, other dimensions that need to be considered: 1) the form of the plan (written and formal vs. verbal and informal), 2) the frequency of updating and recasting the plan (sporadic or scheduled), 3) who needs to be involved in the planning process (multiple stakeholders such as executives, line managers, staff, and customers or a plan that is imposed by executive management); and 4) the linkage of the strategic and financial plans (estimating the implications of strategic options to the bottom line). These are important considerations when planning.

What we also know is that an uncommunicated strategic plan is unimplementable. Once the plan is formalized in writing, circulated to key administrative staff, generally agreed upon, and included in the organization's marketing materials, a systematic plan review-and-revision process is required to ensure that initiatives are evaluated and assessed and organizational goals are achieved (Armstrong 1991; Bryson 2004; Hax and Majluf 1984; Keller 1983).

The earliest approaches to strategic planning and strategy followed the simple and informal model of Mintzberg's design school, which focuses on a non-complex model that perceives strategic formation as a process to reach a satisfactory balance between internal distinctive competence and external threat and opportunity. This approach was much more detailed and tactical in nature in Ansoff's book *Corporate Strategy* (1965). In the book, strategy formulation is deconstructed and the work assigned to a series of subunits that follow intricate procedures as determined by an extensive group of planning specialists. In this approach, strategy tends to emerge as a series of tactical techniques organized by department with analytics underlying its performance.

More recent forms of conventional planning tend to conceptualize the plan from an internal viewpoint by focusing on problem-solving. In many cases, and as an abbreviated check for rationality and a way to connect the plan to the company's competitive markets, organizations attempt to view the nature, appearance, and appropriateness of goals and strategies as well as performance measures through an external lens (Rowley, Lujan, and Dolence 1997).

Okay, that's the path organizations have trod right up to our doorstep. Now, what do you need to create strategy *today*? Let's first consider what tools are needed in our strategy toolbox.

Strategy Tools

SWOT Analysis

Most organizations follow a system when planning. This normally means adapting a readily available plan that includes frameworks, forms, tools, and structures for their particular situation. In practice, the planners gather information on the organization's **Strengths**, **Weaknesses**, **Opportunities**, and **Threats**, the output of which is commonly referred to as a SWOT analysis. This initial assessment can be relied upon as a time-tested framework to gather information from interviews, planning documents, performance reports, industry and competitive analyses, and other sources of data in order to better understand how the organization measures up, both internally and externally, to its competitors and in their industry. The report involves specifying the objectives of the business venture or project and identifying the internal and external factors that are favorable and unfavorable to achieving those objectives. It includes an evaluation of the organization's core competencies (operational strengths and weaknesses), a study of the competition (competitive analysis), a study of the marketplace (industry analysis), an evaluation of internal and external challenges to its goals (threats), and a summary of potential goals (opportunities).

According to Porter (1985), to be effective, a SWOT analysis must be augmented by a systematic, follow-up process that is designed to monitor and adjust the plan when necessary. Once the planners have the needed information, they can begin to understand the organization's strengths or what they do particularly well, and in the case of weaknesses, what they don't do well at all. For example, an organization may have very strong technical expertise and at the same time have an ineffective marketing program, or sales staff may sense a new opportunity involving the expansion of an existing product line but simultaneously identify a much larger competitor with aspirations to move into that same product area. So, what's the point of this work?

As an assessment tool, the SWOT analysis focuses inward, helping leaders better understand an organization's competencies. It's used to specify the goals of the business venture or project clearly and objectively and to identify the internal and external factors that are favorable and unfavorable to achieving those goals. Strategy research has found that plan review needs to be done at regular intervals using a systematic approach, and at least annually at the departmental level, and when this process is followed, is a leading indicator for operational success (Armstrong 1982).

PEST Analysis

Now that you've completed the SWOT analysis and know a lot more about your organization's internal preparedness and competencies, what's next? It's time to take a look at those external forces that will affect where you choose to locate your business, what forces beyond the organization and competition may need attention, and how to include these findings in your plans. For this work, we use another tool in the strategist's toolbox, the PEST analysis, to identify **P**olitical, **E**conomic, **S**ocial, and **T**echnical external threats. The PEST is a systematic approach to understanding what threats exist that are out of the organization's control but could be critical to its success. Similar to the SWOT, the PEST analysis brings discipline and objectivity to the organization's assessment processes, in this case, to external threats. For example, a technology company could be planning to take software development offshore to lower labor costs and speed up product development, but encounter significant headwinds in the form of country policies that heavily tax that kind of approach (Political), or exchange rate issues that would cause significant repatriation taxes on any profits (Economic), or there could be labor unrest in target markets making the staffing of factories difficult and expensive (Social), or there is a lack of high-speed internet in the town or cities where the technical staff are located (Technology). By utilizing a PEST analysis, the technology company would better understand the challenges related to the location of key facilities and be better prepared to make objective decisions.

Porter's 5 Forces

Michael Porter is one of the most recognizable names in modern corporate strategy and corporate competition. Developed at the Harvard Business School in the late 1970s, Porter's 5 Forces model is believed to be the gold standard in industry analysis to determine an industry's attractiveness and likely profitability. It is widely used to describe how organizations develop and maintain a competitive advantage, and while some criticize the relevance of Porter's model, saying it is too slow and irrelevant in today's fast-moving corporate world, I disagree. As a framework and structure, the 5 Forces model is a very useful tool for planners in all industries. While not a "one-size-fits-all" prescription for success, the model, along with Porter's research and writing, are a treasure trove of ideas that anyone working in the area of strategy, planning, competition, and organizations must make part of their business toolbox. Here's how Porter's 5 Forces, and the rest of the strategy models, fit together.

After the organization has completed the internally focused SWOT and the externally focused PEST analyses, it is time to answer the question: How does the organization know there are opportunities and profits to be made in that industry? By utilizing Porter's model, organizations are able to evaluate the industry in which they endeavor to do business. It attempts to evaluate the following:

1. **Competitive rivalry—likelihood to come out on top of the competition.** Understanding competitors informs direction related to the four Ps: price, product, place, and promotion (e.g., customer acquisition strategies, needs, etc.).

2. **Supplier power—reduce or manage.** A diverse supply chain allows for price competition and reduces supplier risk, resulting in lower costs and increased dependability for products and services.

3. **Buyer (customer) power—reduce or manage.** The number of customers relates to the power they hold over the organization. More customers mean less organizational power, and fewer means more.

4. **Threat of substitution—reduce or eliminate.** If the product or service is unique and difficult to copy, the threat of substitution is low, and the inverse is true.

5. **Threat of a new entrant—reduce or eliminate.** If competitors can easily enter the market and compete effectively, the organization's position is weak. Strong, durable barriers to entry make the organization's position strong.

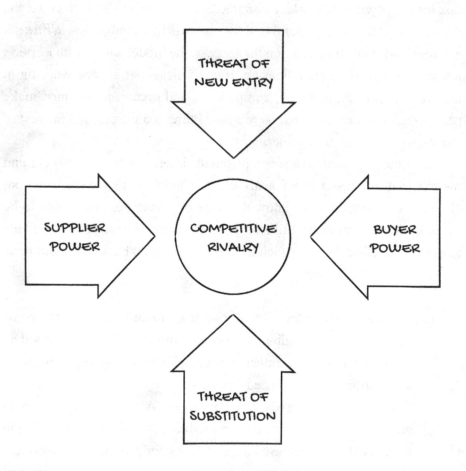

Porter's 5 Forces analysis identifies and categorizes the key and permanent sources of pressure within an industry, with the caveat that we do not confuse them with other more dynamic and temporary factors such as growth rates, governmental actions, and technical innovations. Recently, however, this approach has been criticized. While it is true that the model includes, among other things, a significant effort involving data gathering and analysis, and as a result has been criticized for being backward-looking, like SWOT and PEST, these are the best-in-class frameworks for evaluating the strategic forces at work in order to look ahead. It is safe to say that no framework, template, or process is able to predict the future. The 5 Forces analysis is the next step for planners after the SWOT and PEST. Organizations will be well-served to use these tools to systematically and objectively review the organization's internal capabilities, external conditions, and industry profitability before launching off into new businesses, products, or services. Planners need structure to make sense of the past and create scenarios of the future, and up to this point, these tools work best.

Strategy's Primary Goal

Competitive Advantage. In two words, that's it.

Michael Porter wrote the book on competition and competitive advantage, and since his books are popular and widely available, we don't need to go into this in detail. His generic strategies, which can be applied to products and services in all industries, were published in 1985 and offered a simplified way to understand and categorize strategies and approaches tied to competitive advantage, defined as "the leverage one business has over another in the same industry" often gained by "offering better products and services at a superior value" (Porter 1980). What follows is a brief description of Porter's teaching related to competition and competitive advantage and how that relates to strategy.

Organizations have the option to offer products and services based on the four Ps of marketing: price, product, place, and promotion. So, why does a consumer fly Delta rather than United, stay at a Hilton rather than a Hyatt, or drive a Chevy rather than a Toyota? The consumer makes choices based on the four Ps, plus their own economic situation and preferences, and the battle to influence those choices is at the heart of competitive advantage. Defined by Porter as the leverage a business has over its competitors gained by offering better and greater value, he explains that competitive advantage can be achieved in two ways: cost advantage and differentiation advantage (Porter 1980).

Porter's interplay between the generic strategies of cost (no frills) and differentiation (unique and desirable products and services), along with a third focus (a specialized product or service in a niche market), can be applied to organizations of all sizes and industries in order to gain an edge or advantage. He suggests that a cost strategy may be achieved by either reducing production costs and/or reducing production costs while increasing market share by charging lower prices. The trick in utilizing a cost strategy is the ability to lower costs while protecting your market leadership and, therefore, the price you can charge. In a differentiation strategy, organizations create different and more attractive products and services as compared to the competition. It involves differentiating features, functionality, durability, and support along with a differentiating brand image.

Executing a differentiation strategy requires strong product research, crisp product development (Agile), continuous innovation, the ability to deliver high-quality products and services, and an effective sales program to sell the differentiated products and/or services into productive sales channels. A focus strategy concentrates the work of the organization on a niche market by deeply understanding the market and its customers and then developing specified and often unique products for that market. Due to the limited nature and size of a niche, organizations successful in these strategies can dominate the niche and minimize competition. The focus strategy works well for smaller organizations without the resources or talent to deliver at scale; it allows them to focus on one segment or value-added feature. The challenge with the focus strategy is making sure these niches are large enough, in and of themselves, to support the organization.

Generic strategies apply to all kinds of organizations, including nonprofits. While familiar with using a cost strategy that minimizes the cost of obtaining donors and donations, and a differentiation strategy based on the specific work of the nonprofit, a focus strategy makes sense as a way to get donations from targeted individuals and foundations interested in a small category of needs and programs. Choosing which strategy to deploy underpins the rest of the organization's work supporting every decision, so taking the time to get it right is time well spent. Porter warns to avoid "hedging your bets" by trying to utilize more than one generic strategy since each of the strategies appeals to a specific audience under a particular set of circumstances. Cost requires an internal focus on efficiency and processes, while differentiation demands external-facing creativity and adaptation.

Porter's competitive cost leadership strategies are more deliberate and, therefore, linear in nature as compared to Hall and Tolbert (2005) and Wheatley's (2006) entrepreneurial strategy, which is more emergent or chaotic; the Miles and Snow (2003) typologies that argue defenders are more deliberate than analyzers; and the Mintzberg and Waters proposition that different types of strategy blend into one another in different contexts over time. Deliberate strategies are planned, methodological, and prescriptive, stressing direction and control; emergent strategies lend themselves to the notion of strategic learning, adaptation, and change. Mintzberg and Waters stress that emergent strategy does not mean chaos but rather a kind of unintended order and conclude that "strategy walks on two feet, one deliberate, and the other emergent" (p. 271).

A more thorough understanding by researchers of the relationships between the types of strategies and how they perform in different contexts would be beneficial, both to the study and the practice of strategy.

PART 2:
Figuring Out What to Do

Chapter 5

HOW CORPORATIONS AND UNIVERSITIES PLAN

Is Strategic Planning Relevant?

While there is common knowledge that strategic planning is one of the initial activities of organizations when they launch or where they look to when evaluating performance, markets, and opportunities, there has been a long-standing debate in strategy circles on whether or not strategic planning is a valuable process, with a number of scholars lined up on both sides: that strategic planning is increasingly important, particularly in these complex twenty-first-century situations, and others suggesting that planning is useless, when considering the speed of business and information and communications in contemporary organizations.

As I will explain in greater depth later, my own experience while launching and operating a business showed me that creating a strategic plan, discussing it with my staff and customers, and using it as a guidepost for decision-making and measuring progress and performance was incredibly useful. That form of planning, and that process, would be unlikely to yield similar results today as the business environment is incredibly different but the underlying principles of planning remain relevant and useful.

As described earlier, when I was working at a large research university, all four deans and the three presidents had different points of view about the value of strategic planning. They ranged from "I'm not interested in planning" (ironically, from a dean who was a strategy scholar), to an education school dean who said, "I don't want to put the faculty through another planning exercise," to a practicing consultant who was new to higher education and brought his corporate approach to planning by leading the organization through a very detailed, constructive, and helpful process. How is it possible that within one institution, the seven leaders with whom I worked had such different views regarding the value of this activity?

I've been amazed at the people I have worked with who have little interest in strategic planning and don't value its use and some who outwardly disdain its mention. The simple fact is that while Mintzberg and Porter went through periods of acceptance and criticism, they evolved their points of view regarding the value of planning over the course of their careers. So, if you want a consistent answer to the question "Is strategic planning still relevant?" you're out of luck. You'll have to study the topic, decide for yourself, and live with the consequences. For me, the answer is yes, and the research supports my position.

In the *Harvard Business Review* article titled "The Rise and Fall of Strategic Planning," Mintzberg said, "Organizations disenchanted with strategic planning should not get rid of their planners or conclude that there is no need for programming. Rather, organizations should transform the conventional planning job" (Mintzberg 1994). He suggests that it is critical for the contemporary planner to be positioned as the leader of the planning process by selecting team members, specifying the research needed to create smart scenarios, and then acting as the coach for the planning team, acknowledging that there is "no one right answer." By defining the planner's job as such, their work is less about process and more about strategic thinking or from analytics to the ability to break down a goal or set of intentions that can be implemented almost automatically. Planning, as a process, has always been about *analysis*—about breaking down a goal or set of intentions into steps, formalizing those steps so they can be implemented almost automatically, and articulating the anticipated consequences or results of each step. Planning as a strategic activity becomes part of how the organization operates, part of its culture. Developing this capability in an organization is the planner's most valuable contribution. By redefining the planner's job and supporting the work from the executive level, companies will be acknowledging the difference between planning and strategic thinking and encouraging staff to embrace the latter.

Criticism of strategic planning isn't limited to practitioners, as many scholars share this sentiment. As mentioned earlier, Henry Mintzberg wavered between advocacy for the value of strategic planning and as a critic. He became increasingly critical of strategic planning, suggesting early in his career that it was a critical and valuable activity, and later that it was an overly bureaucratic, pseudo-analytical process that lulls managers into believing that by developing a plan, they could expect outcomes and high-level performance (Mintzberg 1994). While Mintzberg was inconsistent in his criticism of the strategic planning process, he, along with many others, criticized it and suggested more sophisticated processes were needed.

On the other hand, John Bryson, another strategy scholar who focused his research on higher education, suggests in chapter 1 of his book, "Why Strategic Planning Is More Important than Ever," that strategic planning can help leaders and managers of public and nonprofit organizations meet their goals by developing a process consisting of "thinking, acting, and learning, strategically" (Bryson 2018). Supporting Bryson's point of view, Martinez and Wolverton agreed that strategic planning is valuable if for no other reason than as a coordination activity that is strong at building consensus at the rank-and-file levels (Martinez and Wolverton 2009). Interestingly, they also mention that when viewed as a linear *process*, planning can minimize the value of "intuition" by stifling innovation and creativity.

In my experience, planning for organizations of varying sizes, industries and level of resources differs significantly. Robert Bradford, CEO of a strategy consulting company, reports: If you feel you can see trends unfolding five years into the future, it would not be unreasonable to do your strategic planning with a five-year horizon. However, if the future gets very murky just a few months out, you should consider a different approach. There are three workable approaches to strategic planning in a highly uncertain environment:

1. Use a very short planning cycle—revising your plan every three months, six months, or one year.
2. Have shorter strategic planning meetings quarterly, and constantly update and revise your strategies.
3. In situations where there is high uncertainly about a possibly catastrophic outcome (i.e., health care reform in the medical insurance industry), create scenarios of the two to three most likely outcomes and plan around each.

Some practitioners and scholars disagree on the definition and purpose of a strategic plan. For me, companies without a strategic plan are akin to someone taking a trip without a map. How do you get from point A to point B without knowing where you're going? Would a map, by itself, limit your options as to where to turn right and where to turn left? No. What it does show you are several ways to get to your destination. Strategic plans work in much the same way. They provide many options (e.g., roadways, bridges, alternate routes, etc.) to go from point A to point B, and strategic plans attempt to do the same. They provide a pathway the organization can follow, and as the situation changes (e.g., if there's a wreck or a back-up), faster and less crowded alternative routes can be considered.

Strategic plans are also valuable as a signaling device to both internal and external audiences regarding the organization's mission, vision, and values. For internal audiences, it is useful as a communication device that maps out strategic direction and outlines priorities so staff, investors, and customers interested in the company know where it's headed. For external audiences, the plan can be a valuable communication tool that portrays organization, focus, and direction. How many of you reach for the mouse and google individuals and companies prior to taking a meeting or during the due diligence process? All of us! Knowing that, organizational leaders need to use this important communication channel to share the specific messages he/she wants to share with these audiences.

Finally, strategic plans create accountability for the leaders who create and follow them. It is this last purpose that some leaders do all they can to avoid. As you will see in the following section that describes planning in corporations and higher education, a number of leaders do all they can to distance themselves from a plan and their responsibility to deliver specific results.

Planning in Corporations and Higher Education

Corporations

Up until very recently, strategic planning and strategic management were most closely related to corporations. Go to a website or read an annual report. There will inevitably be mention of mission, vision, values, and goals, with the report content focused on annual goals and the company's performance. Since the nuts and bolts of strategic planning are well described in many other books and referred to in a number of the case studies elsewhere in this book, let's pivot this discussion to the use of scenarios. Utilized during World War II, researchers on behalf of military leaders developed game theory and decision analysis techniques that were, after the war, transferred to business and industry. These "scenarios" were refined in the 1960s at the Hudson Institute to help people break through mental blocks related to the "unthinkable" (e.g., life after a nuclear war). At the same time, Stanford was operating the Strategic Research Institute (SRI) with the goal of offering long-range thinking for businesses that combined operations research, economics, and political strategy with the military and hard sciences. In these exercises, scientists attempted to predict the future (e.g., undersea communities, commercial passenger rockets, and expansive nuclear power) without consideration for the economics of markets. While most of the predictions were wrong, what this new approach to planning did find was that predicting outcomes was more complex than formulas and calculations could manage and that the attempt to identify the variables and model outcomes was a worthwhile step forward in the art and science of prediction and planning (Ringland and Young 2006.).

In the late 1970s, at the RAND Corporation, Herman Kahn pioneered the "future-now" technique that attempted to use detailed analysis plus imagination to produce a written description of what life would be like in the future. Named the "Delphi technique," the goal of this new approach was to mathematically estimate the probability of certain events in the future, becoming part of the formal planning techniques of this era.

In the late 1960s and 1970s, the SRI Futures Group began a project commissioned by the US Department of Education (USDOE) using numeric forecasts and literature searches to create four potential scenarios and one "official scenario" related to the Future of American Society in the year 2000. While the official scenario was referred to as "status quo extended," essentially an extension of a normal state over multiple decades, the other four were much more volatile and, in some cases, disruptive and violent. While the researchers predicted the "New Society" scenario as most likely, the USDOE disagreed and shelved it. One positive benefit from this work was the development of a free-flowing process that encouraged the development of original thinking and idea generation, or asymmetric learning. This concept is the cornerstone of a newly developing approach to planning proposed later in this book. During this same time period, Systems Thinking entered the planning picture and added to this work by attempting to use a feedback loop among five key variables: population, food production, industrial production, pollution, and natural resources, the interactions of which are still loudly and energetically debated today.

In the late 1960s, researchers sought corporate support for their work, and companies like Shell, GE, and IBM began to work in this arena, with Ted Newland leading the discussion about the future at Royal Dutch/Shell

(Shell). With computers starting to enter the planning picture, corporations used a top-down approach, creating models, forms, and charts to visualize their predictions. Shell Group led the way. For ten years after WWII, Shell relied upon its planning work and predictions to justify expanding and setting up new facilities around the world. These activities were primarily scheduling-related, relatively stable and predictable, but risky and expensive, nonetheless.

Bringing Strategy and Finance Together

In addition to prediction-based modeling, Shell developed a technique called Unified Planning Machinery (UPM), a computer-driven system that brought more discipline to cash flow planning. It was designed to plan for a whole chain of activities to occur, from discovering oil in the ground to offering it for retail sale to consumers within a certain time frame. Shell planners understood that the surprise-free environment they enjoyed in oil production would not continue and that new, substantial players would be entering the field, particularly from the Middle East. By bringing scenarios together with financial models, the company had a vision for both the supply chain and the financial implications of different ways based on different conditions and outcomes. However, Shell executives, realizing that UPM was limited to a six-year time horizon, tended to get a lot wrong and decided to discontinue that program.

Following the UPM project, other Shell executives began an activity called Long-Term Studies, targeted at scenario development and longer-term planning. Named the Year 2000 Report, long-term outlooks were less about prediction and more about linking strategy, innovation, risk, and leadership development into one single and continuous process. Still in use today, Shell continues to evolve the approach to help shape its global thinking about energy and other matters and, at times, its strategy (Wilkinson and Kupers 2013).

As you can see, scenarios are an important tool in the planner's toolbox. During the recession of the late 1970s and early 1980s, strategy scholars suggested it was time to return to scenarios as a way to better understand market forces, get ahead of trends, and use sensitivity analysis to guide their work in increasingly volatile global markets. As a result, firms contracted for and consultants developed new scenario methodologies, including Intuitive Logics, Trend-Impact Analysis, and Cross-Impact Analysis, to name a few. The 1990s were a period of resurgence for scenario planning with a new emphasis on discovering new sources of value and growth as Prahalad and Mintzberg, the leading strategy scholars of this era, encouraged firms to look outward for strategic context and the need for strategy in light of the turbulence ahead.

Higher Education

"Just as metaphors of war, battle, and aggression—first among corporate organizations and then in the academy—bring to light the military-style leadership principles abounding in strategic planning, so the widespread embrace of 'agility' uncovers a strong desire among academic leaders to act more quickly, without cumbersome processes and restraints."
—Richard Utz, *The Chronicle of Higher Education*, 2020

Strategic planning at colleges and universities is, on the one hand, unique and, on the other hand, typical of large, multiproduct line, multinational corporations. Because the underlying strategic planning research project for this book focused on higher education and intercollegiate athletics as its study population and proposed certain dimensions of planning that became the basis for a new model of planning, a brief description of the uniqueness of the higher education industry and the challenges related to planning is called for.

Before we dig into higher education, planning, and strategy, it is worth acknowledging that these institutions are populated with talent functioning within a unique and challenging structure: faculty tenure. In no other industry in the world is the labor force guaranteed employment. This distinction is important as we compare planning and management in higher education with other industries and organizations. While this book will not address the benefits and challenges of tenure per se to the extent it affects planning and strategy, we will.

How does tenure affect planning and strategy? As my higher ed colleagues can confirm, the existence of tenure has seeped its way into every institution at every level, with many having little stomach for corporate-style goals and objectives. In practice, there are few if any incentives tied to productivity or program success, and little chance that poor execution and performance will result in a firing. Performance goals, timelines, and consequences are simply not part of the higher education lexicon.

A slightly different take on tenure, one that affects the institution's commitment to planning, can be found in the president's office. Since the average tenure of a college president is less than five years, when these leaders are appointed, they are charged with ambitious and often short-term programmatic and financial goals. Since the time window is short, these new leaders often bring familiar key staff along to go faster and make changes, resulting in the layering of new staff positions on top of existing ones. Often referred to as "administrative bloat," this process, resulting from short-term thinking, results in sclerotic and unmotivated organizations being left behind when the leader inevitably moves on. Here is one infamous example.

In one case study, when the new institutional leader arrived, he inherited an institution with a storied history, large endowment, high demand for its programs, and enthusiastic and dedicated alumni. His priorities included initiating a strategic planning process, improving diversity among the administration, faculty, and students, and launching and overseeing a multibillion-dollar capital campaign. Having worked at the executive level at both business schools and experienced firsthand the staff and systems in place at the institutional level, what he also inherited—but wouldn't be aware of until months later—were antiquated management information systems; an organization designed to manage a smaller, perhaps less entrepreneurial and ambitious portfolio; and an entrenched administrative staff that had little to no incentives to rise to the occasion, take on more responsibility, and support his ambitious agenda. What could he do? He could dismantle the current organizational structure as one might at a corporation, weed out and fire the under-performers, and bring in new people committed to his programs, an extremely time-consuming and traumatic process for any institution, or simply bring new staff on board and rebuild and reassign roles and positions. He understandably chose the latter, and while this certainly had the potential to quickly make change, it was neither the most financially prudent nor did it fix the root cause of the institution's inefficiencies. And what would be left behind in what was likely a five-year term?

As an example of what is sacrificed when making short-term versus long-term leadership decisions, these short-term leaders don't have the time or the incentives to really get at the underlying issues that are often holding back the institution from achieving its full potential. These institutions are unable or unwilling to make the changes necessary to modernize and prepare for a much more volatile and dynamic twenty-first century. With that as context, let's take a look back at the evolution of strategic planning in higher education before we look ahead.

The Evolution of Strategic Planning

In the 1990s, the American public became increasingly discontent with the government in two areas: education and personal safety. Public approval of the government fell as economic insecurity became a new concern for millions of Americans. In a 1997 study by Hartle and Galloway, they reported an acute concern for the future by reporting that colleges and universities were entering a period that would fundamentally transform what they did and how they did it. At the same time, the Clinton administration committed to balancing the federal budget, which resulted in sharp cuts in federal spending for research. The combination of public discontent, a sense of insecurity, and predictions that higher education was headed toward significant change was the backdrop for institutional leaders, and planners and planning, entering the twenty-first century.

From 2000 to 2008, much of the Republican effort focused on shifting responsibility for programs to state and local levels. Congress, state legislatures, and boards of trustees demanded that institutions demonstrate their effectiveness in return for continued funding. One way for institutions to do this was to formulate strategic plans and conduct a continuous assessment of progress with an eye toward the achievement of their stated goals (Dickmeyer 2004; Voorhees 2008). Planning techniques found to be successful in the business sector began to appeal to a wide variety of organizations such as not-for-profits, governmental agencies, and increasingly, colleges and universities (Rowley, Lujan, and Dolence 1997). The benefits for higher education were obvious, as were the criticisms, with general agreement that institutions needed to quickly get up to speed on every facet of planning, from conceptualization and scenarios, through measurement, goal review, and flexibility and adjustment.

Due to long-standing traditions of shared governance and decentralized management, alternatively described as "political" (Baldridge 1971), "anarchic" (Cohen and March 1974), and "loosely coupled" (Mintzberg 1985; Weick 1995; Wilms and Zell 2002), the challenges to implementing an integrated strategic planning process in higher education were daunting. These slow-moving institutions found themselves clinging to survival strategies as globalization and technology exerted increasing pressure requiring that they act more entrepreneurial and businesslike. Rapidly changing policies and funding models, along with the significant and continuous alteration of the environment in which these institutions operate, and calls for accountability, access, and affordability, created a new and treacherous view of the future (Chaffee 1989; Hartle and Galloway 1997; Raines and Leathers 2003; Tierney 1999).

The world of higher education today is not the world of its origin. In the past, planning procedures used at colleges and universities failed to pay adequate attention to their environments, were slow to develop and modify, and have been deemed no longer relevant. In the words of a colleague, "universities are slow-moving ships that don't change course at the whiff of new ideas and new ways of thinking" (Pusser 2008). Due to long-standing traditions of shared governance and decentralized management, universities faced unique challenges to reliance on an integrated and activated strategic planning process with attempts to deploy these modern management techniques a source of anger among the faculty and administrators (Mersen and Qualls 1979). However, there are a number of studies that suggest strategic planning and higher education can, in fact, co-exist, and here is one. Collier (1981) developed five elements of strategic planning specifically related to higher education that remain valid today:

1. Strategic planning is a determinant of the future of an institution.
2. The entire planning process is composed of both the formulation and implementation of strategy.
3. Strategy decisions require matching the particular institution's characteristics and resources with its environment.
4. Strategic planning requires that the institution determine its own future.
5. Planning decisions should be synergistic with the goal of improving organizational flexibility.

All of the above elements are as valid today as they were in the 1980s. How can these elements be adapted to today's era of rapid change and adaptation? How should institutions manage a process that can be both valuable and disdained by a large swath of its stakeholders? How can institutions use incentives and accountability to move the academy toward more contemporary approaches to strategy? Perhaps a good crisis is needed. Let's take one quick look back to a time when a creeping crisis entered the operational considerations that forced institutions to consider more organized approaches to how they conduct their business.

During the 1990s, and in response to decreasing state and federal support, growing market pressures, and boards of trustees and public policy demands for greater accountability, most institutions began to engage in some form of strategic planning. In its earliest forms, institutional planning could be described as loosely coordinated, subunit-driven, and incremental with a lack of agreement on whether strategic plans should be developed by the subunit and fed upward, with the administration consolidating them into an institutional plan, or whether there should be an administratively prescribed process to which the individual units respond (Presley and Leslie 1999). Either way, the signal was clearly sent, and as a result of the Great Recession of 2008–2009, institutions needed to follow battle-tested planning programs to avoid being hurt by the next crisis. Little did they know that an existential crisis, the pandemic of 2020–21, was on the horizon. In the corporate world, executives are less concerned about whether pushing a plan up from below or driving one from the top down is optimal. Instead, they ask what the return on their investment is for taking the time and spending the money to create and manage a plan.

The same questions hold for start-ups and growth firms. Companies often assign, designate staff, or hire a consultant to drive the planning process. While this makes sense in the short run, assuming the goal is to get a plan in place, there is no consideration for the ongoing reliance on and benefit of the plan's utility as a guide and tool to organize a continuous strategy evaluation and portfolio review process.

Many scholars and leading practitioners suggest that the higher education industry is slowly coming around to seeing the utility and benefits of taking a more businesslike approach to managing these complex institutions. There is growing support for the notion that if new education models are to succeed, there also needs to be significant business model innovation (Salisbury 2019).

As we will see later, the directionality and frequency of communications up and down the organization, along with the design of feedback loops, are of critical importance to the successful deployment of twenty-first-century planning programs. While the studies described in the preceding chapters all serve as background and foundation for building an understanding of planning in general, the question still to consider is whether any are useful in the current dynamic environment. In the two very different industry contexts of corporations and higher education, planning as practiced up until the end of the twentieth century is essentially unusable, indicating a need for a new model that is more flexible, team-oriented, customer-facing, socially responsible, and environmentally aware. My research project, first published in 2010, came to this same conclusion: Due to the speed of communications and the profound business and societal changes resulting from technology, a new way of doing business was needed. It became obvious that a new era of dynamic and Agile strategies was needed. This book is one step in this attempt to examine the planning process in order to guide institutions, executives, and managers by suggesting how to plan, when to plan, and what to do in the planning process.

Contemporary Planning

> *"A model is only as good as its underlying data,*
> *and data in a time of extreme uncertainty, such as*
> *a global pandemic, presents a serious challenge."*
> —Charumilind et al.

The use of scenario planning is widespread and on the rise. In a 2007 Bain & Company study, two researchers reported that the firm's regular survey of management tools showed an "abrupt and sustained surge" in the use of scenario planning after 9/11. Although there have been ups and downs since then, another Bain & Company survey showed that 65% of companies expected to use scenario planning in 2011 and beyond. Forward-looking models are nothing new. The insurance industry, weather forecasting, stock market forecasting, and manufacturers' production estimates all use a type of scenario planning or interactive, multivariate model in their work. The scenarios or models can be used for sensitivity analysis to measure the cause and effect of a range of select variations in production and sales on financial outcomes and the supply chain. They can show how even small changes in key assumptions can produce large variations in outcomes (Charumilind et al. 2020). For planners, having a tool that can distill scenarios into an automatically generated set of outcomes is incredibly valuable.

In 2020–21, as a result of the COVID-19 pandemic, scenario planning was being used to prepare for future disruptions as never before, particularly in higher education. The massive financial losses related to what is likely to be either a hybrid or online fall semester, along with an uncertain spring, the loss of room and board, executive education program revenue, and other auxiliary services being limited or eliminated, is driving campus executives to create dynamic models of the '21 operating plans and budgets. In Paul Friga's (2020a) article, he describes three steps for creating a plan designed to guide an institution through this period of disruption and turbulence ever to hit higher education. Interestingly, his number one suggestion is Scenario Planning. He encourages higher ed planners to establish best and worst-case scenarios for 2021 and then plot several variations in between. For Shell, they developed six or seven scenarios when they planned, while others developed three.

In higher education, using Friga's 2x2 diagram below, with "Minor v. Major" (effect on revenue) on the x-axis and "On-Campus v. Online" (locations for program delivery) on the y-axis, and depending on the institution's capability to deliver classes in multiple modes (online, hybrid and in-person) and the severity of the problems, planners can find structure, logic, and recommendations as conditions unfold. In this way, scenario planning can consider the effect of enrollment drops on finances; or whether or not there is, or should be, a football season with all its auxiliary revenue; or whether or not international students, typically full payers, are able to return to campus.

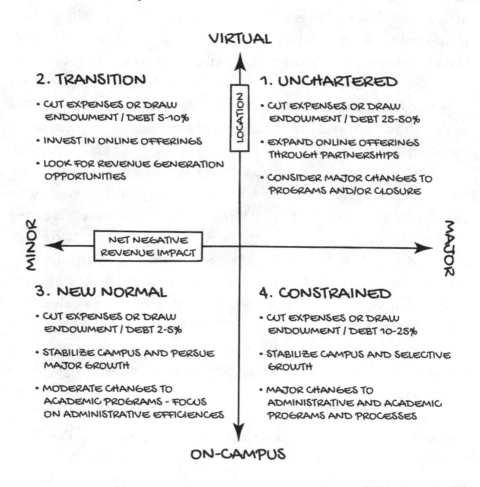

In the corporate world, scenarios continue to be used to model various conditions and the effect on cash flow and profitability. Recently, according to McKinsey, the pandemic has forced companies to revise pre-pandemic strategies and budgets to meet the new normal with a sharp increase in the number of organizations using scenarios to manage the uncertainty of the current situation.

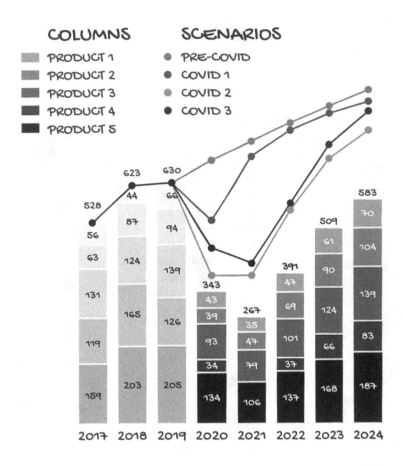

Another display developed by McKinsey, the "uncertainty cube," is designed to capture thousands of scenarios much like the Monte Carlo simulation and run them against the income statement and balance sheet to estimate a wide variety of possible situations and expected financial effects.

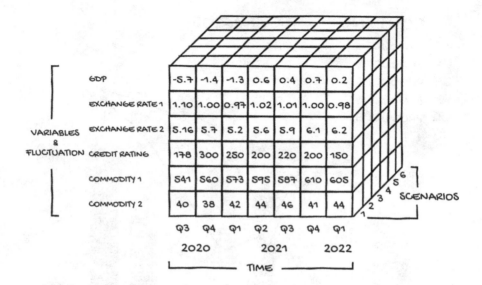

These tools can be run at the subunit, unit, and company-wide levels or at the local, regional, national, or global levels, with each selecting the approach that best fits their individual situation. If the balance sheet withstands these stress scenarios, it is more likely to hold up under scenarios that are more likely to materialize (Grube et al. 2021).

Once stories are developed for each scenario and operating models are developed and functional, developing assumptions and decision-making points need to follow. What is critically important for institutional leadership is to have the necessary data to make informed decisions. The more dynamic and well thought out the models, the more likely decisions will be seen through the lens of long-term consequences. While the McKinsey study incorporated a large number of companies, and those lessons are certainly valuable, let's drill down and take a closer look at a smaller nonprofit using scenarios in their planning program.

The Adirondack Futures Project: Scenarios in Action

It took quite a while and a lot of digging to uncover a ready and detailed example of a scenario used in planning that could be shared. In conversations with consultant colleagues, they said companies rarely offer up their frameworks and proprietary approaches and require non-disclosure agreements to be signed prior to beginning any work. Luckily, I discovered the Adirondack Common Ground Alliance's ADK Futures Project that, among other artifacts, has a functional website and reviewable materials, reports, and progress measures available to the public at ADKfutures.org. The ADK Project started in 2011 with a series of scenario workshops that focused on the "desired future," or "Endstates," for six strategic priorities: A: Wild Park, B: Usable Park, C: The Sustainable Life, D: Adirondack County, E: Post "Big Government" Solutions, and F: The Adirondack State Forest (see Exhibit 2a in References). After the initial workshop, each of the six Endstates was described in detail (see Exhibit 2b), analyzed for desirability and feasibility (see Exhibit 2c and 2d), and then broken down into discreet categories, including dates of data entry and timelines (see Exhibit 2d).

In the final step, or phase, labeled "Endstate Synthesis," results are tracked and synthesized and then displayed in a graph (see Exhibit 3). This is a terrific example of how the scenario process works, what kinds of reports are useful, and how the scenario-planning process can be used to guide decisions, inform legislation, and communicate goals and progress to a wide array of stakeholders.

In the next couple of decades, scenarios are likely to be used more often as business professors and MBAs become increasingly adept at understanding and applying the potential, along with newly developing technologies that allow for faster surveillance, to a varied set of corporations and industries. Using the results of more traditional analyses and methods, such as SWOT, PEST, SMART, and Porter's 5 Forces, when combined with scenarios and automation, may be the combination of approaches that bring planning out of the dark ages and into the light of interactive, team- and customer-generated, asymmetric modern plans and results. In a recent article that relates scenarios and planning, Nakano proposes that while it may sound antithetical to Agile, a bit of planning can increase competitiveness. Once you have identified ten drivers of your business, there are four steps to follow:

1. Create ten scenarios by imagining what happens as each driver activates. For example, one could be that a high unemployment rate might drive the need for lower-cost suppliers, and another might be a low unemployment rate and higher-cost suppliers.
2. Choose two to four scenarios you think are most impactful and plan for them.
3. Build out three- to four-page stories along with your responses.
4. Set up a tracking system that provides dashboard indications if and when any of the scenarios emerge (Nakano 2012).

Clearly, contemporary conditions, including hyperfast and ubiquitous communications, technological advancements, and globalization and competition, make the development of new approaches to strategy formulation and implementation a top priority. The slower, less interactive methods of planning are simply no longer acceptable.

Finally, the public and NGO sectors in the EU are using scenarios to harness the energies of their members. In the private sector, scenarios are taught in workshops to create a common language or as a learning tool for management teams (Ringland and Young 2006). As we explore elsewhere in the book, the use of scenarios to draw out the implications of certain actions, to drive mergers and acquisitions, manage portfolios, or to optimally locate a manufacturing plant or distribution centers, will be increasingly valuable. As we plan, we need to develop methods to identify, collect and analyze the variables, and then how to analyze the interactive effects among all of them. What we do know is that scenarios are valuable tools for planners, and they are becoming more dynamic, relevant, and pervasive. How to best manage the process will be discussed in more detail later in the book.

Chapter 6

PLANNING MODELS

As discussed in chapter 1, strategic planning followed a historical pattern, with the earliest examples having characteristics that were simple and linear in nature and practice, well suited for industrial and military uses and contexts. During the mid to late twentieth century, a number of variations in approach began to emerge, having similar but distinct characteristics and better suited for planning as technology quickened the pace of work and companies globalized. These variations were combined to form the hybrid model. In the modern era, scholars and practitioners continue to wrestle with trying to calibrate planning with the speed of business and its changing nature in what has been referred to as the chaos model. These models—linear, hybrid, and chaos—align with the approaches to planning consistent with the needs of organizations from the 1900s to the present day.

Managers and leaders, many of whom have been educated in the 1970s and '80s and having progressed in their careers to executive or leadership status, often find themselves reaching out for frameworks and approaches to use in the creation of strategic plans. Assuming these leaders find strategic planning to be of some value, what they often wrestle with is how to guide their planning teams through the process. While they may know that the process includes understanding the organization's capabilities and competencies and where opportunities exist, they also realize that strategy is developed and applied in a fluid, unpredictable environment, making the crafting of strategy, not the plan, the goal (Kenny 2016).

What we can agree on is that businesses exist in a rapidly changing and dynamic environment, most still operate slowly and deliberately, the planning programs of the past are no longer relevant, plans are guidance tools and not prescriptions, one can expect disagreements about the future and should accept the ambiguity, and that plans are always a work in progress.

That we are stuck in the planning approaches of years gone by should not be a surprise as most executives and institutional leaders were trained at universities and in MBA programs of the 1980s and 1990s at a time when strategy was still emphasizing control and processes as a way to comprehend a chaotic and dynamic world. Leadership teams are now trying to shake off the rust of the past and move quickly into the fast-moving environment of the present while planning for an uncertain and increasingly complex future. One thing for sure: There is no sure-fire, single approach to planning. Each organization needs to consider its situation, markets, and resources before deciding how to move forward. Let's take a look at some of those options.

The Planning Continuum

For planners, one size does not fit all. Planning provides the context for strategy and relies on conditions related to the organization's industry, competition, staff capability and capacity, organizational size and structure, opportunity for growth, etc., with the approach informed by all these factors. Strategy does not equal plan but is rather the process of moving from plan to execution or from linear and comfortable to fluid and uncomfortable. It is about placing bets and making hard choices, with the objective not to eliminate risk but to increase the odds for success (Martin 2014).

As discussed in the preceding pages, models help make sense of the array of multiple approaches developed incrementally over a long period of time. As uncovered by the underlying research study, while each model is composed of individual characteristics, some of these, when added to the characteristics attributed to the chaos or complex model, signal a new way to plan. This new approach, referred to as the complex model in the research, can be best described as "Agile" with characteristics related to Agile project management techniques that include fast-moving, iterative, evolving, responsive, customer-focused, and team-oriented. The complex model bridges the gap between planning and management by linking planning and implementation; the strategies emerge and morph and shift with timelines that are immediate and urgent. Within the complex model are events, called "Pivots," based on events and conditions that cause the organization to move away from one strategy and toward another or the need to discard a strategy and design a new approach to a problem or opportunity.

While Steve Denning, a recognized scholar in the areas of leadership, management, innovation, and organizations, along with other Agile advocates, suggests that traditional planning is essentially dead and has been replaced by Agile principles of implementation that are directed toward and often alongside customers' needs, often disavowing any benefits for the traditional tools like SWOT, PEST and Porter's 5 Forces. Frankly, I disagree with ignoring time-tested tools on three dimensions: 1) Based on the lessons of the past and an objective review of what is happening in organization and industry globally, what is most likely effective is a combination of the traditional tools (e.g., SWOT, PEST and Porter's 5 Forces), to be used as a framework for understanding where we've been, or what Denning refers to as the "rearview mirror"; 2) External scanning of the organizational, industry, and external conditions present provides vital background information upon which to base decisions and directions; and 3) Ignoring the teaching of history in schools or ignoring what has occurred throughout the history of any industry, whether favorable and unfavorable, risks being ill-prepared to address how changes and dynamic conditions present in markets and industries will likely affect the future. While taking this more comprehensive approach makes sense in concept, it's a wonder there is resistance to making the move from more linear and adaptive approaches to one with its principles in complexity theory.

Critics of planning believe that due to complexity and fluidity, there is no value in planning. Uninformed advocates and acolytes agree, or at least don't argue, and off they go into the uninformed and blind bliss. Rather than argue that one's support for planning is an "either/or," either it's valuable or it is not, let's agree that it is a "both/and" proposition, with one end of the planning spectrum a command-and-control or top-down model with top management prescribing desired behavior and dictating strategy (linear), and at the other end is the generative model in which top management abdicates strategic control, and the organizational structure and strategy are formulated and reformulated as conditions and competencies dictate (chaos). Where an organization falls on the spectrum is the result of many factors, including industry, age of the business, competition, competency, etc., and the bias of the leader. It may be useful to take a brief look at the planning models and their unique characteristics to better understand how and why they were developed and utilized and if and how they may be of use in the future.

Planning Models

To better understand the different ways to approach planning, a number of planning models have been developed to categorize and differentiate each. Located somewhere on the history of the planning spectrum between the linear form (1900–1960) and complex forms (1990–Present) are four or more submodels that, because of their relative similarity, are often combined into one and referred to as the hybrid model (1960–1990). The hybrid era is best described as a series of continuous and slightly different approaches to planning, often described as a "continuum of emergentness of strategy" and characterized by the indiscriminate blending of some of the characteristics of other submodels (adaptive, interpretive, emergent, and contextual) into a single model, or "hybrid," making it easier to compare the benefits of each.

Strategy scholars agree that:

1. Several strategic dimensions, supported by research and extensively tested at organizational and corporate sites, underpin these models: intended (what we plan to do), emergent (what we did but hadn't planned for), and realized (what we did and planned for) (Chaffee 1985b).
2. Organizations may have both corporate strategies (What business shall we be in?) and business strategies (How shall we compete?).
3. Strategy is implemented from two operational perspectives: conceptual (the plan) and analytical exercises (the execution) (Hax 1984; Hitt, Freeman, and Harrison 2003; Mintzberg 1994).

As you contemplate your next strategic planning activity, what I recommend is to consider these models or approaches, your organization's capabilities and culture, and the industry and competition before embarking on a major planning program. For example, if your organization is well-funded, stable, and historically successful, an approach that leans more toward linear may be called for, and conversely, if you are a start-up tech company, a more complex model may work best. In order to build an understanding of the characteristics needed to get your planning started, the next few pages will describe each of the three models and how they may be relevant and useful in your planning efforts. But, first, here is a very brief description:

Model 1: Linear
Historically, the linear strategy is the earliest of the strategic planning models and is best described as methodical and prescriptive, direct, sequential, and plan-based following a step-by-step methodology (Chaffee 1989; Keller 1997). Often described as a command-oriented approach, according to Fredrickson (1990) or an engineering and analytical approach, it actively discourages learning and change in the operating parts of the organization

and yet continues to be widely used (Halachmi and Bouckaert 1996). For the linear model to succeed, the organization should be tightly coupled, enabling decisions made at the top to be implemented throughout the organization (Chaffee 1985a; Fredrickson 1990; Mintzberg 1994).

Interest in the linear model waned in the mid-to-late 1970s as strategic problems were perceived to be too complex and nuanced to be effectively addressed in such a one-dimensional manner. However, and particularly in the instances of large bureaucracies like the government and universities, the linear model continues to flourish. Criticized by some scholars as being too dependent on hierarchy, this command-oriented approach complicates communication and collaboration, emphasizes rules and regularity, and discourages innovation and adaptation. While some aspects of a linear approach may still be useful, there remains universal dissatisfaction with linear strategies, though they continue to be widely used (Sherwood 1992).

Model 2: Hybrid

The hybrid model includes characteristics found within at least each of these four other submodels—adaptive, interpretive, emergent, and contextual—located on the strategic planning research continuum. As described above, these four submodels are often combined into one and referred to as "the hybrid model." Historically, strategic planning practices followed a rational pattern beginning with a simple linear model (from the earliest military planning through the 1940s), continuing through a series of incremental and related models (postmodern era, from the middle to the end of the twentieth century), and moving to the contemporary chaos model (twenty-first century). As businesses became increasingly complex, so did strategic planning practices. The planning models, or submodels, included as part of the hybrid model were developed within a limited time span (1940s–1990s), consecutively building upon characteristics of the previous model, making differentiation between them difficult. As Hart suggested, planners should consider different modes, or in this case the characteristics of different models, in order to maximize planning approach design.

Planning takes care, understanding, commitment, and a sophistication in its design and implementation. One size truly does not fit all.

Increasingly, planners found that the models examined in the research and deployed in practice were less useful for what was developing in the late 1990s, a more chaotic and unpredictable management environment. As a result, a movement toward developing a strategic planning practice founded on the principles of complexity theory began, with a fundamental shift away from the rational and predictable models of the past (top-down and later, emergent) and toward a model acknowledging the unstable, diverse, and extremely complex characteristics of modern organizations (Barnett 2000; Wheatley 2006).

Model 3: Complex Model

Finally, modern chaos theory, also referred to as complexity theory, and its application to organizations began in the early 1960s with Kaoru Ishikawa's cause and effect diagram known as the Ishikawa diagram, or "fishbone diagram." This theory, grounded in the concept of causality, suggested that when applying this process to management, people were encouraged to think in observation and feedback loops, rather than in a linear manner, to replace the idea of mechanical causality or linearity, which held that a given cause has one and only one effect (A causes B). While linear systems tend to be conceptualized as the sum of their components, nonlinear systems are thought to be *more* than that, indicating that A and B working together within the same system may create many different and varied effects or that outcomes have multiple or multiplied effects (Morgan 1986). The complex model includes many of the characteristics attributed to nonlinearity into account.

A new planning model is developing, one that is grounded in research and experience, bringing planning and implementation together in one single and continuous process. The integration of Agile principles into this new way of working is the next leap forward in management, allowing for visionary planning, diligent industry and market surveillance, flexible and responsive goals, and energized and accountable executives, staff, and customer teams.

The Origins and Integration of Agile and Planning

"Rather than organization as machines,
the Agile organization is a living organism."
—McKinsey & Company

Senge (1990) was the earliest management scholar to apply a nonlinear framework to organizations, suggesting that information flows up and down and around organizations in a complex and chaotic manner. Strategic planning has also recognized a similar phenomenon in regard to environmental sensitivity and influence (Armstrong 1982). The value of feedback to strategic planning objectives is well documented in laboratory studies and in the field with feedback loops, including market intelligence from the point of sale, critically important to planners and managers alike. Based on this information, as plans are adjusted and investments made, feedback infiltrates the system, allowing it to take advantage of emerging changes quickly and effectively while maintaining order and providing for continuity (Cutright 2001). Chaos theory states, and many management scholars agree, that planning to predict and control is probably illusory and dangerous, allowing for a false sense of security. However, it also states that organizations should embrace an approach that accepts instability and unpredictability by recognizing the principles of strange attractors, self-similarity, and self-organization (Tetenbaum 1998). Duggan (2007) said that in a complex system, strange attractors provide boundaries and general direction that, by default, facilitate decisions consistent with the organization's mission and goals. As the system adjusts to its environment, much like the bee colony or migrating flocks of birds, the organization re-forms by propelling toward self-similarity and self-organization.

It is instructive to apply the principles of chaos theory and their relationship to planning at higher educational institutions. There is interactional complexity to these large organizations; their mission includes creating intellectual capital, applying an increasingly global viewpoint to their work, and coordinating these goals among a diverse and independent set of operating units (Barnett 2000; Cutright 2001). When colleges and universities scan their environments, they often find rapidly changing markets, new networks, and competing interests, resulting in significant uncertainty. By following principles of the chaos planning model, institutions ascribe to flexibility, regular iterative feedback, and plan modification, resulting in the creation of a "planning culture" (Cutright 2001, p. 6).

Ironically, while these institutions are places where competing and often divergent points of view are embraced and openness celebrated—and you might expect the modern university would be open to new frameworks, inventions, and processes—in practice, they operate as parochial, slow to change, and sedentary monoliths (Barnett 2000; Cutright 2001).

As the third decade of the twenty-first century unfolds, scholars have turned increasing attention to complexity theory and its relationship to strategic planning and strategic management theory (Cutright 2001; Wheatley 2006; Tilman and Jacoby 2019). In recent scholarship related to organizations and management theory, a new form of planning is emerging that is often referred to as the "new science," with significant attention paid to scenarios, sensitivity related to possible future states, and increasingly sophisticated dashboards and computation in an attempt to analyze and guide decisions (Rouse 2016). One primary tenet of the new science is that many organizations operate under a number of rather unique conditions and that rapid change pushes them away from traditional planning models and increasingly toward self-organization or chaos. In fact, it is in this chaotic environment that the constant feedback from managers and executives to strategic planning objectives and management decisions is needed more than ever.

Chapter 7

WHAT'S NEW IN PLANNING

There are a number of new ideas and approaches to planning, along with sophisticated platforms and systems that can be used to plan, implement, track progress, and adjust the way forward. Here are a few new ideas related to planning that all leaders, managers, and planners should consider. Detailed descriptions of the available software and systems being utilized in the field are included in a later chapter.

Asymmetry

What's new in planning is asymmetry. Once a vision is shared and a set of high-level goals agreed upon, leadership needs to assemble teams of staff experts to begin designing activities, products, and services that will be of value to your customers in a continuous planning process that drives strategic choices and decisions and becomes, by its creative and innovative nature, part of the organization's culture.

While the "how" of planning is important, the "who" is where creativity occurs and ideas are generated. This process, often referred to as asymmetry and asymmetric learning, is characterized by the assembling of smart teams who, when given a task, often not only solve that problem but uncover other solutions and opportunities that add significant, unexpected value to the organization. Here is why this matters.

Asymmetric Learning

I've spent a lot of time thinking about specific aspects of planning that would benefit from some new thinking and came across an article about asymmetric learning. The author, Mike Rea, CEO of IDEA Pharma, a pharmaceutical industry consultancy, talked about how teams that he works with to run clinical trials often follow a time-tested process that begins by directing a team to design a drug that treats a particular disease, with disregard for other uses that may come from the trials. In a twist to traditional clinical trial processes, he suggested that teams should not only address the original illness or condition but also remain open to other uses for the drug. By eliminating the limitations of a one-problem, one-solution process, he encouraged teams to take note of any and all other uses for these drugs, both intended and unintended. He referred to this as asymmetry and asymmetric learning, and the more I read, the more I realized this idea had great potential in management and planning (Rea 2020b).

Just like the naturally occurring patterns described in chaos theory and those used to describe communication forms and patterns occurring within an organization, the process describing the way pharmaceutical companies are broadening the work of R&D teams in clinical trials allows for the evaluation of the drug for both its intended use and any other use that is useful and commercially viable. Having its basis in science, asymmetry—when applied to planning and management, and organizational complexity—suggests that when humans attempt to comprehend complex situations that include factors such as competition, environment, industry, political, technical, and societal, there is often stress between the linearity of modern planning and management processes that operate in an environment of unpredictability. In the face of uncertainty, leaders, planners, and managers often attempt to manage emergent and complicated problems using tried and true linear planning systems that simply do not work in this complex context. As a result, humans need new ways of dealing with complexity.

In what Margaret Wheatley calls "The New Science," she suggests that a useful metaphor for planners to consider is that of a biological system that ebbs and flows in an unplanned but orderly way, leading the system to new and unique conclusions, much like how collections of individual snowflakes accumulate into piles of snow or individual leaves when connected to branches become part of a tree. This accumulation of individual biological interactions, when applied to organizations, can help explain how individual bits of information, interactions, and activities, which are often outside the control of the planners, when left to self-organization and nature, often result in the discovery of new pathways and new and unexpected results. For planners familiar with linear processes that include task and activity logic, lists, and diagrams, this lack of linearity is a challenge that needs to be addressed. The real opportunity for planners and planning can be found when linear thinking makes way for asymmetry where the learning happens on its own and teams learn to adapt and adjust to change.

Asymmetries, in the form of organizational knowledge and information flows, occur naturally and can be leveraged to the organization's advantage with bundles of properties, people, and relationships apt to be unique in countless ways. Indeed, many sources of learning occur (e.g., including long-term contracts and distinctive forms of knowledge consciously created), but many asymmetric capabilities also emerge, including systems thinking, new and improved skill sets, and smoother and more nimble processes, often the result of adapting to unpredictable forces and events. Many of these asymmetries are complex, subtle, and persist even in the face of market, institutional, and competitive pressures (Noda and Collis 2001). The key to asymmetric learning is to create organizational designs that get the right parties collaborating, to create reward systems that encourage "asymmetry-exploiting" behavior, and to build and monitor information systems that detect relevant asymmetries and the opportunities they provide (Miller 2003). Social network analysis is one such system. There are many others.

Miller's study of some two dozen firms shows that their sustained successes were less about building on resources and capabilities and much more dependent on asymmetries, defined as skills, processes, or "assets" a firm's competitors "do not and cannot copy at a cost that affords economic rents" (p. 201). These rare and non—substitutable assets, while not directly related to any value creation, often act as liabilities for the firm attempting to copy or mimic. By discovering and recognizing these asymmetries and then embedding them within the organizational design and leveraging them across appropriate market opportunities, many firms in the study were able to turn asymmetries into sustainable capabilities (Miller 2003). The challenge to planners and leaders is to design ways to operationalize these capabilities.

According to Rea, when you apply this perspective to the work of teams and planners, it helps increase our understanding of how teams, when given a task and some autonomy, are able to not only evaluate the assigned task but are likely to leverage their efforts by uncovering new and innovative ideas. These "accidental successes" or "serendipitous events" often result in new, innovative, and advantageous ideas, products, and services. He asks, "Can serendipity be planned?" The answer is yes and what follows is how this works (Rea 2020b).

Imagine you give different teams, comprised of members with different expertise, the same set of conditions or variables and task them to develop a specific product or solution to a problem. In every case, you can expect different outcomes. For example, in the world of pharmaceutical R&D, when the planned outcome of the trial is different than the results, the drug is thrown on the dead pile and, in most cases, never heard from again. In the asymmetric approach, if these teams were tasked with the planned outcome but also had the freedom to follow other options with the potential for "pleasant surprises" or other uses for the drug and these "surprises" were evaluated as useful and commercially viable, then the team and the company would Pivot away from the planned use and toward the uses for the drug that hadn't been planned for or considered. One example of how this approach resulted in the serendipitous discovery of a new product is the story of Viagra. Originally targeted for hypertension, the drug was initially labeled a failure but later was found to address erectile dysfunction. In the pre-asymmetry world, the drug would have been labeled a failure and discarded. However, in the world of asymmetry and possibilities and serendipity, Viagra was discovered to address a different important problem and developed into the $2 billion per year juggernaut drug it is today.

It is important to note that applying an asymmetric approach to projects is heavily team-dependent, with leaders responsible for approving the overall direction, allocating needed resources, and removing barriers so teams can work. Heavily dependent on smart, flexible, and well-trained staff that are given a task or set of goals and encouraged to contribute to a process of continuous ideation, this process often results in new ideas or insights. In this contemporary brand of strategy, the activities we refer to as "planning" and "management" are coming together in a new and continuous process where planning leads to insights, insights lead to strategies, and strategies lead to new products and services. Add on performance measurement, and the cycle is complete. No need to separate planning and managing. If we accept that planning is continuous and flexible and that planning is part of strategic management processes, then we also should accept that planning and management, as understood for the last hundred or so years, has profoundly changed, and something new has taken its place. This concept of asymmetry is core to this newly developing science called Agile management.

Rea suggests that often, "accidental success" or "serendipity" can play a part in the discovery of new products, that organizations and teams can "plan for serendipity" by creating environments that continuously generate insights, and that in an environment of inherent uncertainty, the potential to exploit the ideas developed by smart teams, both by design and as a result of serendipity, needs to be embraced and not ignored (Rea 2020a). Wheatley and Cutright described a similar process they call the "New Science" in the early 2000s and beyond Wheatley's New Science is an even "newer science," which is the gaining of competitive advantage by empowering teams, providing resources, removing barriers, and then being pleasantly surprised at the outcome (Wheatley 2006).

Asymmetric Planning

Over the last decade, planning has changed from a linear process that attempts to predict the future to one focused on the shorter term where teams work together to solve the customers' problems and then integrate, test, and pilot solutions. Planners work side-by-side with project managers to eliminate any misunderstandings that can result from the plan to implementation handoff. Customers join the process by adding their own needs and those of their customers. Leaders need to accept that development processes designed to solve one specific problem may head in multiple directions, spinning off new products and services that are often very different than what was originally proposed.

Planners need to recognize and accept unpredictability and randomness. In fact, the spontaneity of brain waves and neural networks serve as better metaphors for organizational planning than do roadways or process diagrams. Just as information flows in social networks toward people (depicted as nodes) with deep expertise, experience, and trust and not because of a predetermined reporting structure, so too do the market conditions, expertise, capability, and opportunity begin to converge, pushing and pulling firms along. Setting a target and then evaluating and tracking options and pathways while remaining open to pivoting toward new opportunities requires smart staff, flexible leadership, and a keen awareness of the organization's surroundings, competition, and competencies. Preparing for this randomness while also providing soft structure is worthy of more discussion.

Using Biology as a Metaphor for Planning

In another example borrowed from the natural sciences, scholars in the IT and Agile world compare the iterative idea generation of the planning process to that of a cell splitting into other cells through mitosis. At the start of the project, a problem is identified, or a product is proposed that needs definition, development, and testing. By building smart teams, providing resources, and allowing the team the freedom to generate multiple options, the original task will not only be delivered, but new, potentially break-through ideas and options, often far removed from the original proposition, are also generated. This asymmetric learning is a key to the Agile organization. Here is what the mitosis diagram looks like:

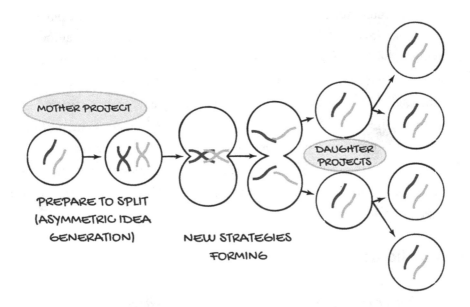

In these seemingly random systems, "Roadmaps" can be used to determine the product plan, the implementation plan, and funding for the initiative quickly and effectively. Using this framework, teams can determine a budget and resources needed for the project, start earlier, deliver faster, increase customer satisfaction, reduce risk, and realize benefits sooner. They also put the customer at the center of the initiative, so the solution directly meets their needs and reduces the planning time and cost by more than 50%. By following the principles of Agile planning, when combined with Agile management, teams often finish and pilot projects in the same amount of time normally allotted for traditional planning methods alone (Robinson 2020).

Another approach to planning that can be even more spontaneous and creative is the Riot Games approach described in the SD Learning Consortium's 2017 report. In an exercise whose goal was to develop a learning process related to the development of new interactive video games, the process was divided into two dimensions, strategic and tactical, with each broken down into five components or process steps: 1) vision, 2) impact, 3) strategy, 4) outcome, and 5) output. The goal was to focus on the outcomes needed to achieve certain impacts (SDLC 2017). In this "let's imagine what we want to be first in and then we can decide how to get there" approach, by working in teams to create vivid visions of the future, and then identifying and analyzing strategic options, the planning exercises generated new ideas that, when coupled with a "vivid descriptor," became the north star for their self-organizing teams and part of the company's vision. It seems like scenarios and visioning—activities often associated with traditional planning processes—remain the frames through which modern developers still see their worlds.

Unpredictability

"Emperors, explorers, and presidents made decisions without
fully understanding either the situation they faced
or the effects of their actions. And so must we."
—John Kay and Mervyn King (2020)

Because of inherent unpredictability and variation and the hundreds, possibly thousands, of variables in most projects and programs, current planning models fail primarily due to the false optimism of preprogrammed outcomes and a lack of commitment by the planners to work the program and consider a range of outcomes. What we know from the cases in the drug industry is an acknowledgment that unpredictability is ubiquitous and, as such, needs to be allowed for when humans are making decisions and creating plans. Rea describes this as the "prediction paradigm," suggesting that while there are unknowns, there are also unknowables, making prediction impossible (Rea 2020). One recent example of dealing with unpredictability comes to mind. At the start of a day-long planning exercise at the Darden School of Business, the facilitator, an alumnus and chief strategy officer at a consumer products company, set expectations by acknowledging unpredictability. He encouraged participants to imagine what they know (predictable), the future of the graduate business school industry, and what each thought was possible for Darden (unpredictable, but possible). By framing unpredictability in this way, we didn't waste time trying to predict the future but instead imagined a trajectory of change in the industry (vision and scenarios) that we needed to keep in mind as we sketched out a short and longer-term plan.

Another example of how to think about unpredictability can be found in the book *The Black Swan* by Nassim Taleb. He describes a black swan event as "the impact of the highly improbable" and suggests that while on the one hand, these events may be improbable, on the other, they are possible and should be considered when planning (e.g., the Great Depression, the Plague, 9/11, the Great Recession of 2008, the pandemic). He goes on to say that the biggest lesson from past black swan events is the need to prepare, suggesting that three phenomena are working simultaneously—unpredictability, extreme impact, and a deliberate bias—to explain it away, all working against what some perceive as the value, or lack thereof, of planning (Taleb 2020).

In several meetings with planning teams who spent way too much time worrying about how to predict the future, I advised them to stop worrying about the false precision of predication and more on imagining a generalized and realistic vision of a future state. Being "directionally right" by finding your market niche, imagining outcomes at different levels of success, and being ready to Pivot when opportunities arise is much more likely to yield consistent positive results. For those who want a clear and precise vision of the future, you'll be disappointed. Like the map and route corrections metaphor, organizations can be guided by planning but should not assume that following plans will result in predictable outcomes. These roadmaps provide direction and require attention and adjustment. They need to be systematically reviewed and adjusted as part of the regular business routine in order to be of any real value.

Another way to think about the development of business routines, including, among other things, the uncovering of opportunities and adjusting of strategic directionality, was discussed in a *Fast Company* article, which used the COVID pandemic as the subject of a "problem map," developed by researchers at Vanderbilt University. These maps helped uncover hot spots and potential opportunities for infection spread reduction and were used by groups charged with tackling the multiple, interconnected problems caused by the virus. The map is a helpful tool as it reveals and diagrams system interactions, feedback loops, and conflicting agendas that, according to Terry Irwin, Director of the Transition Design Institute, "can be barriers or boons to wicked problem resolution" (Peters 2020). So why not use similar maps for planning?

Imagine if planners and planning teams used what Peters calls "multi-level perspectives" (p. 2) and scenarios as the basis for diagrams and used the diagrams as tools to better understand the what-ifs, future risks, and potential paths forward for each? Why can't that basic idea be applied to planning? If nothing else, the "problem map" can be useful as a postmortem tool capable of helping planners understand what happened, where and how those affected are connected, and how to plan for future events. Like all database-like tools, the information can be translated into trend data and will get increasingly predictive over time. It certainly seems worthwhile to invest the time to analyze trends and anticipate potential outcomes in order to develop solutions and uncover opportunities. By purposefully identifying potential challenges ahead and remaining diligent with observing the organization's activities and performance and the industry and competitive trends, this approach could go a long way in addressing small issues before they develop into wicked, systems-wide problems. When strategies, progress, and external trends are fed into a planning system designed to automatically create a problem map, multiple outcomes can be analyzed and directions adjusted quickly and consistently. This planning system automation is a glimpse into the future of strategic planning and, when shared with operations and project management teams, serves as the launch point for Agile management!

Taleb suggests that preparation is the remedy for uncertainty, not more precision, and Rea suggests that when organizations ideate and evaluate, they move from prediction to the development of hypotheses, "if-then" statements, and vision and action pathways. Both agree that when organizations make use of plans in this way and design a planning process that encourages this kind of thinking and learning, they will be doing something useful. This is where the opportunity lies.

How to Sharpen Your Approach to Planning

Let's circle back and consider how to sharpen planning activities that drive the organization toward smarter, better, and more effective and responsive management practices. Once an organization has documented its strategic plan and is underway, new projects and products are proposed that require design, market analysis, and financial review. Guiding these planning efforts is the organization's mission statement that describes why the organization exists, what product or service it provides, who its customers are, and where it operates. It can function as the filter through which any new products and services must pass before moving these ideas to the planning team for evaluation. In my experience, if a new project is inconsistent with our mission, we will pass on it. Full stop. No need for discussion. If a proposal is consistent with the mission and has promise, it is then moved to the planning team for evaluation. Here is a diagram of how that works.

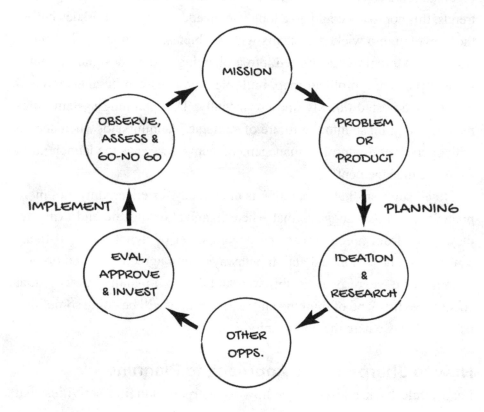

In this new Agile approach to planning, the planning team needs to evaluate the financial potential and IT, regulatory, economic, and business risks. There are multiple stops along the proposal cycle for review and approval. Since the organization's executives and its customers are involved, funding is already in place and ready to go at the end of the analysis.

Once the product or program is approved and the proposal is passed to the management team, the establishment of feedback loops needs to be a top priority. Using unbiased performance measures that are decided upon before the project moves into the field, managers are able to assess progress and determine where they should spend their time and money building capacity and increasing market share and where they should disinvest and move on.

Once the product is in the field and the feedback loops are operating, planning teams should allocate time to review the progress and, if necessary, work with the management team to consider other solutions to the customer needs and other potential uses for the product or service. Planners need to remain part of the process to ensure the customer problems are solved and, where possible, to bring new ideas to the table for consideration. In more linear approaches, these new ideas are often ignored as the team's focus is often limited to designing a particular product or solving a specific problem, with no interest in considering alternatives. As a result, there is no learning, discovery, or innovation, no planned (or unplanned) serendipity. New drug discoveries like Viagra and Lipitor would have never been discovered had the R&D goal been limited, singular, and narrow in scope and focus. Planners should heed these lessons and encourage the project teams to be on alert for new, unplanned outcomes. Once new ideas are uncovered, collected, and approved as new projects or initiatives, there needs to be an equally responsive product delivery/project team ready to take the handoff and move these new products and services from planning into the field. The next section will describe this new approach, called Agile management, in more detail.

Chapter 8

PLANNING AND COMPLEXITY

*"Today, you need real-time data, real-time monitoring,
and real-time alarms when trouble is brewing—not lag-time
metrics that hide the real issues for 24 hours or longer.
Your business should operate like a nuclear reactor. If a
problem arises, you need to be aware of it immediately."*
—John Rossman

Complexity Theory and Planning

Contemporary organizations and leaders find themselves operating in an era of profound change and increasing complexity. During the early twentieth century's Industrial Age, organizations were modeled and managed within a top-down structure, with most of the work focused on creating value-added products from a less valuable set of raw materials and labor. Industries that dominated the corporate landscape were in the oil and gas, automobile, and consumer products industries with names like Ford, Texaco, and General Electric.

In the energy business, oil and gas discoveries were plentiful, with the challenge being the moving of fluids and gas from the field to the end users. For the car manufacturers, many of the innovations were in the areas of raw material sourcing and manufacturing efficiency. In the consumer products industry, innovations in the manufacturing of inexpensive products and packaging, along with efficient assembly, were the areas of focus. They analyzed efficiency and developed systems used to track productivity and reported to management simply and consistently. For example, steel mills, a major industry in the age of industrialization, would receive huge quantities of low-cost iron ore by ship and rail. They would then process those materials in large preparation yards and move those materials through the mill, stopping at departments called "Melting" and "Shaping" and "Cutting" and "Welding" and "Cleaning" and "Painting" and "Delivery." These custom shapes, weights, and lengths of steel would then be bundled together and trucked to a worksite to be erected as a building's structural framework or to a fabrication plant for further refinement as ornamental and decorative metals. The economics of these processes were based on the purchasing of raw materials at low cost, managing the supply chain to obtain, ship, fabricate, and then bring the finished goods to market, hopefully at a profit.

Following the lessons learned from continuous-flow processing lines in place at meatpacking companies and mills throughout the US, car manufacturers at the turn of the twentieth century, beginning with Ford's moving chassis assembly line in 1913, designed moving lines for the assembly of parts built in the factory and sourced from direct supplier purchases. The individual parts, in and of themselves, were not very valuable. However, once assembled, the cars that rolled off the assembly plants in Detroit were not only more valuable (and more expensive) than the sum of their parts, but these machines changed generations of lives forever.

In this example of early strategy, companies converted raw materials, individual parts, and assemblies into more useful products that added cost and increased value along the entire supply chain. Companies focused maximum effort on applying efficiency and scaling techniques in order to transform raw materials (inputs) into market-competitive products (outputs) as fast and as low cost as possible. The coin of this realm was maximizing efficiency, managing the supply chain, and controlling the cost of raw materials. By doing so, companies captured market share and gained a competitive advantage. This simple approach to strategy in industrial settings was less and less relevant as industries became increasingly complex and global.

In the twenty-first century, the world has become increasingly educated and its organizations more advanced. First-world economies have evolved from the industrial form to the knowledge form, and as a result, are becoming increasingly complex, global, and interconnected. Some organizations are adapting to this new set of conditions, and some are not. Some are taking advantage of this period of rapid change, and some are not. Virtual offices, teleconferences, and instant communication comprise the language of these new companies, often multinational and global in form and function.

In the case of Dell, their laptops are an assemblage of parts sourced from parts fabricators in 140 different countries, shipped to and assembled in China, and then direct shipped all over the world. In this organizational structure, office locations don't matter. Salespeople are calling on clients across the globe. They enter orders into a central database located at the home office in Round Rock, Texas, and simultaneously, orders are converted into fabrication instructions that are communicated to various assembly plants throughout the world. Once the products are assembled and tested, the finished goods are shipped directly to the clients' locations. No one from Dell ever touches the parts or the finished products.

Most product companies follow the Dell model and have developed the same production, assembly, and direct ship approach to their businesses. If you are a manufacturer, partnering with Amazon has to be part of your strategy. If you are launching a new company or expanding an existing one, pay close attention to supply chain feedback and customer requests because those are the signals upon which you will base the next investment and the next set of strategic initiatives.

This is the context in which leaders of organizations operate. Some leaders—and therefore, some organizations—are adapting to this new set of conditions. Some are not. Certainly, institutions like higher education, religions, healthcare, and banks are not immune. In fact, those industries are learning lessons that may be instructive for others.

Consider Institutions for a Moment

In a recent and well-publicized episode of the clash between slow-moving, incremental, and dynamic strategies, a university president was forced out because, as the critics suggested, she was an "incrementalist" and not "broadly strategic." The board members were interested in a new leader whose focus would be on "strategic dynamism" and "agility." Whether the efforts to oust the president were warranted or not is the subject for another day, but the questions related to organizations and strategic management and disruption remain. What changes should leaders of these old-line, historical, and traditional institutions make to adapt to these new conditions? Knowing they will be criticized for resisting change and ignoring both competitive pressure and economic reality, how will they evolve and develop some modicum of strategic agility? Is this an existential threat, or can they continue to plod along? For most institutions (e.g., higher education, religions, and banks), the answers are: Yes, they need to change, Yes, all are threatened, and No, they can't just continue with business as usual.

The fact is colleges and universities are under tremendous pressure from a combination of conditions. These conditions include reduced state support, activist boards of directors, unsustainable levels of tuition increases and student debt, increasing upward pressure on faculty salaries, the aging of the faculty, demographic shifts resulting in increased competition for fewer high school graduates with the means to pay full tuition, and the potential for revolutionary program delivery alternatives such as online and other instructional technologies. It is industry disruption on a grand scale. The sooner these institutions develop more agility and increase their strategic dynamism, the better, or they risk floundering or getting run over by the ambitious large publics and ambitious for-profit competition.

In the case of banks and financial institutions, the competition from online loan providers and the rise of cyber currency has most financial institutions unglued, with some declaring that cyber currency will be irrelevant, despite a recent report from Cornerstone Advisors suggesting that over 15% of US citizens currently own cryptocurrency and 17% more are projecting they would buy some in 2021. In fact, after disparaging Bitcoin, Jamie Dimon, J.P. Morgan's CEO, announced the launch of its own cryptocurrency, JPM Coin (Dimon 2019).

So, while the future may be uncertain, planners at these institutions must take these disruptive changes into account. Where are the risks at your company or institution? What allowances are you making for the future? What are the risks?

Risk and Uncertainty

"If there's one thing that's certain in business, it's uncertainty."
—Stephen Covey

Since planning is an activity with the primary goal of understanding and then developing hedges against future risk, some discussion of how risk and uncertainty relate to planning is called for. While we can agree that trying to predict the future is fool's gold, there are reasonable methods we should incorporate into our plans and planning.

Accepting that the world is full of uncertainty is the first step in dealing with it. From a leadership perspective, the first thing a good leader needs to do is recognize that they don't have all the answers and that they need a strong advisory team around them who they trust to tell them when they are wrong. With a strong team in place, leaders can manage risk and uncertainty by embracing Agile Planning and Management techniques as a hedge. While we all can agree that the world is uncertain, the world is still full of planners who assume things are stable and predictable and that as long as enough effort is put into planning, successful outcomes will result. This is simply untrue.

What we do know is that Agile assumes the opposite: that change is inevitable, that the future is impossible to predict, and that by using Agile planning techniques, organizations can manage the short-term and prepare to adapt or Pivot to the longer term. In the process, Agile teams need to accept that decisions and judgments are much more nuanced and pliable than absolute and that episodes of uncertainty begin within the team and extend to customers and users.

The good news is there are tools available to help guide you in this work. One such tool is the Scaled Agile Framework (SAFe). When combined with Agile principles, planners and managers can create discipline and structure by 1) providing guardrails and the confidence that decisions comply with Agile principles and 2) serving as a rulebook or instructions that must be followed.

> *"Fortune favors the prepared mind."*
> —Louis Pasteur

For many Agile team members, particularly those younger and less experienced, risk and uncertainty are daunting and unsettling. Most need and appreciate structure and certainty. When you add in the tendencies of human behavior, including the likelihood that people change their minds and/or don't behave according to plan, no wonder it is hard work to scale this or any other rational planning and management processes! How do we get started if this is so complicated? By getting back to basics and following Agile principles. Hire smart team members, focus on the customer, iterate and innovate rather than follow a plan to a predetermined conclusion, and progressively pilot and test new products and services (Girvan 2020). Get back to basics. Focus. Simplify. Once your team builds the "muscle memory" to work in this way, they will be prepared to tackle the uncertainty of the future. For many industries, uncertainty and complexity aren't looming ahead but are, in fact, already here.

Disruption, Disruption Everywhere

> *"Learning and innovation go hand in hand.*
> *The arrogance of success is to think that what you did*
> *yesterday will be sufficient for tomorrow."*
> —William Pollard

In addition to technological and hypercompetitiveness, uncertainty and risk often add to or drive disruption. As defined by *Webster's Dictionary*, disruption "is to cause something to be unable to continue in the normal way." Harvard's Clayton Christensen builds on that definition by adding that disruption is a term that describes the way in which new entrants in a market can upend, unseat, or "disrupt" established businesses. "Disruptive Innovation" is a term that describes how businesses, both those doing the disrupting and those disrupted, can spot opportunities and threats and act upon them. In response to industry disruption, businesses need to evaluate their business model for relevancy, repeatability, and scalability by observing what is and isn't working in the current business model, orienting the business to the new facts, deciding what needs to change, and then act quickly and decisively (Blank 2010).

A current example of disruption can be found in the higher education industry and the effect of online technologies and instruction. The latest data from National Center for Education Statistics' Integrated Postsecondary Education Data System (IPEDS) shows that in the fall of 2018, more than 6.9 million students, or 35.3% of students in the nation, were enrolled in distance education courses at degree-granting postsecondary institutions versus 25.9% in 2012. Are students adopting online learning and finding it satisfactory? In short, yes. According to an annual survey by Wiley Education Services, 2020 Online College Students, Comprehensive Data on Demands and Preferences, 78% of online students who have learned in a face-to-face setting feel their online experience was the same or better than their classroom experience. Overall, 79% of those who completed their online degree agree or strongly agree that their online experience was as satisfactory as a residential alternative (Statista 2021). So, those in higher education who criticize those who predict meteoric change in this industry, take note. Disruption is clearly underway and driving forward. These questions remain: What will the future of higher education look like five, ten, or fifteen years down the road, and how can institutions prepare as the inevitable takes hold?

It is important to remember that 1) not all disruption is innovation, 2) disruption is market-size and customer-base agnostic, an ongoing and fluid process, and 3) not all new entrants will disrupt. As we described above, higher education is in the early stages of disruption, which is not only profoundly changing how classes are taught but also how institutions will restructure in response to the changes. For example, in 2018, Starbucks, Walmart, and Amazon announced an agreement with Arizona State University and the University of Florida to provide multitier employee assistance programs that focus on vocational certificates or associate degrees in areas as diverse as commercial driving, nursing, and computer-aided design. Amazon hosts their classes on-site in classrooms located within their warehouses.

In another example, eight colleges announced a new collaboration with Google to offer computer and data science courses to its undergraduate students, with the company collaborating on course content, teaching methods, and grading. The goal of the program is to prepare students for careers in machine learning and data engineering with students working in teams with students from colleges and universities all over the US and under the mentorship of Google engineers and faculty from the host institutions. The students attending the pilot program have taken courses in Google's Applied Computing Series. According to Scott Galloway, a former Silicon Valley engineer turned business school professor, this current wave of higher ed disruption will cause the development of a "few, elite, cyborg universities that will monopolize higher education," including MIT@Google, iStanford, and HarvardxFacebook (The College Fix 2020). How long will it be before Amazon or Facebook goes into the higher education business? What this means for the rest of the higher education industry can only be described as "disruptive" and "monumental" in scope and scale. That, my friends, is the textbook example of an industry disruption!

Disruption is certainly not bad news for those outside of traditional higher education. In this brave new world of partnerships between content generators, delivery platforms, and commercial outlets, universities will be able to dramatically expand enrollments by offering online and hybrid degrees in most subject areas and disciplines at an affordable price with the potential of "seismically altering the higher education landscape forever" (Walsh 2020). The current reality for most colleges and universities is this: If Harvard or Stanford, or any of the recognizable, dominant higher ed brands, decide to dominate the market by offering degrees at various levels and in a variety of subject areas, they can do so and put most others out of business. Under these circumstances, how do those, except the elites, plan for the future?

As found in the disruption and sustainable innovation literature, higher education operates in an environment that depends on their product—teaching—to remain proprietary and unduplicatable. The introduction of a widespread disruptive technology—online learning—combined with increasing demand for more education at a lower cost will increase the pressure to extend institutional reach into new markets. Because of the development of new delivery methods (e.g., online and Self Organized Learning Environments [SOLE]), the future of the industry remains unclear. What we do know is that for any institution to survive, it will need to develop dynamic methods for the delivery of its products and programs requiring sustainable innovation and investment. For many, they will simply not be up to the task and, as has been widely reported in the media, the mergers, acquisitions, and closings have already begun.

In a conversation with my dissertation advisor a decade ago, I suggested that higher education was headed into a period of intense change and institutional shakeout. His response was, "Gerry, higher ed is a slow-moving organism, so don't think rapid change is on the horizon anytime soon." Well, I think he either wasn't seeing things for what they were or didn't want to, but for certain, there are still those who believe that higher education is, by design, a slow-moving and deliberate industry unlikely to change anytime soon. However, for the rest of us, accepting that these disruptions are causing the higher education industry to reconsider how it produces and delivers its products with little to no clear vision of how this will be operationalized in the future, preparing for rapid change is the only logical and strategic path forward. Yet, despite this period of rapid change with new and imminent threats on the horizon, some leaders, unfortunately, will choose to ignore this inevitable period of extreme dynamism, only to find themselves and their colleagues standing at the dock while the for-profit, online, multi-programmatic, international, and interdisciplinary ships sail away.

Industry disruption is alive and well in medicine and health care. In a 2011 Harvard Medical School commencement address, physician and author Atul Gawande spoke to the graduates and their families about a similar state of disruption he observed in the medical field. He compared the relative "busyness" of interns in the early- to mid-twentieth century and their minimal effect on patient outcomes with medicine in the twenty-first century and its specialization and lack of cohesion, adding that industry stressors such as insurance company intrusions, government regulation, and malpractice litigation were amplifying the need for balance in the lives of practitioners. In all this, he was describing a state of complexity, driven by industry factors, that doctors need to confront in order to thrive in an environment that has profoundly changed how medicine is practiced. Dr. Gawande found that in 1970, the typical hospital patient consumed the equivalent of 2.5 full-time, clinical-staff days spread among doctors and nurses; whereas, in the 1990s, that number had risen to more than fifteen days. The assumption is that it is even larger today. In his opinion, this network of specialists "will have enormous difficulty achieving great care." By their training and very nature, doctors are becoming cowboys; they are increasingly insulated and self-directed. From this picture of patient-care management, two fair questions arise: "Who is actually in charge of directing patient care?" and "How does this relate to management and strategy?"

Gawande uses a race car metaphor to describe the needed changes in medical practice. Specialist networks, he said, are being transformed into configurations that look and act far more like "pit crews of care." His point is that today's care providers, who are operating more like a system and less like a disparate collection of specialists, actually deliver better care at a lower cost. That is, these teams work together by directing their expertise toward the common goals of the patient. For organizations of all types and sizes, this same approach holds true. Teams working together, focused on a product or service, need to focus on the goals of the customer and consumer. Gawande suggested that this kind of system-level change can be accomplished by using data related to both the successes and failures in patient care as a systematic and objective way to design systems and inform actions (Gawande 2007). Businesses operate in much the same way.

In another example, this same data-driven approach is consistent with what corporate career counselors are asking of business schools today: Teach complicated business analytics so that the school's recent graduates and the firm's most recent hires are better able to develop a deep understanding of and familiarity with the frameworks and systems necessary to recognize business patterns, make decisions, and lead organizations in today's vividly complex business atmosphere.

Organizations need to address the question: How do we scale these processes in order to replicate solutions? There are some underlying theories that will help us better understand how this rapidly changing environment affects planning, management, and leadership. Leaders need to be aware of the unique and challenging conditions they are facing and develop the frameworks and knowledge available to help them cope. And management needs to focus at the systems level and not on individual departments or operating units. Let's look at a few management-related ideas and theories that I found valuable as I prepared to lead a planning exercise.

PART 3:
Understanding Increasingly Complicated Contexts

Chapter 9

MANAGEMENT AND COMPLEXITY

As you create plans, you also need to think about implementation. How can managers manage when information is flowing at a crazy fast speed and competitors are coming out of the woodwork with new ideas and products that relentlessly push us to improve and change? Fortunately, there are a few complexity-related management approaches that will provide the context and depth of understanding for you to distill, decipher, and move forward with the needed speed and information to focus on success.

Management and Complexity

Among scholars, the term "chaos" implies a set of chaotic external conditions that create a series of orderly and comprehendible patterns. Chaos theory is concerned with those instances when doing the obvious does not produce the obvious result (Gleick 1987; Senge 1990). As organizations become increasingly complex, their activities and actions become increasingly similar to biological systems, or those occurring in nature, rather than a planned or managed system. The movement toward developing a strategic planning practice founded on the principles of chaos theory began in the early 1980s and proved to be a fundamental shift away from the rational and predictable models (top-down and bureaucratic) and toward a model acknowledging the unstable, diverse, and extremely complex characteristics of modern organizations (staff, stakeholders and customer inclusion) (Barnett 2000). Scott (2008) proposed that "things happen around an organization that cannot be foreseen" or planned for, making this model very appealing in the highly complex and rapidly changing environment of the early twenty-first century (p. 216).

Sometimes referred to as complexity theory or nonlinear dynamics, the study of chaos theory began when a few scientists in the United States and Europe began to explain how to find order through the study of disorder or find order in chaos. In the mid-1960s, mathematician Benoit Mandelbrot relied on patterns and shapes for problem-solving rather than the traditional formulas. He studied the effect of small, constant change on cotton prices and the symmetry between small- and large-scale events. The Mandelbrot set of images was both an explanation for infinite complexity and a study in paradox: the connection of simplicity and complexity (Gleick 1987; Lorenz 1993; Parker and Stacey 1994).

In the 1980s, Stephen Hawking at Cambridge University recognized that natural laws were inadequate when attempting to explain particle physics, and MIT meteorologist Edward Lorenz (1993) also considered the principles of chaos theory when he published studies of the weather and weather patterns. Lorenz noted that when a number of weather conditions were entered into a computer, and when he modified the patterns by rounding the mathematical formulas to three decimal places instead of six, the patterns began to vary greatly from original findings to the point of little or no correlation at all; that relatively small changes in the formula could cause profound effects. He also noted that boundaries still existed within these chaotic systems, with patterns emerging that demonstrated extreme sensitivity to initial conditions and influx.

Most recently, writers interested in decision-making and complexity include references to biologic systems as metaphors for and examples of information flow on teams and organizations. They reference the self-organizing nature of honeybee colonies, snowflakes, and seashores—and I want to add another. In a recent paper, Professor Suzanne Simard suggests that trees talk to one another and communicate via a vast, messy, and complex underground network of fungal connections called mycorrhiza. In what she calls the "wood-wide web," these fungi are intertwined and reliant on one another to function not only by accommodating tree-to-tree interaction but also between neighboring plants. Similar to what is described in complexity theory, millions of pathways that can go in all different directions form a pattern over time. This mass of natural interacting components is really an expansive network of interrelationships, much like you might find in complex organizations and human systems (Gabbatis 2020).

In Julia Hobsbawm's book *The Simplicity Principle* (2020), she explains that humans can't help but try to manage increasing amounts of complexity, mostly unsuccessfully and often resulting in anxiety, stress, and depression. What she refers to as the CAT syndrome, or **C**omplexity, **A**nxiety, and (too little) **T**ime, is her way of describing the situation when it is virtually impossible to think straight while facing something one doesn't understand. Her remedy is to follow her Simplicity Principle suggesting to 1) keep it simple and 2) learn from nature. While her book explains the value and relationship between the two, when she says, "we can learn from nature and science in order to use patterns in a simple way to process," for our purposes, this concept fits nicely with my proposal that information within organizations flows in randomness that, ultimately, forms patterns just like biologic systems.

While we will discuss chaos theory and planning in more detail later in the book, know that complexity can be simplified, randomness takes the form of patterns, and executives need to recognize patterns and then shape them to be effective. The future is not quite as random as you might think.

According to the chaos theory, small changes within systems will produce great and unpredictable results. The future does not follow trends established in the past, nor will the future simply be a linear extrapolation of the past. Small events occurring today will create new patterns later, with seemingly random activities and systems displaying complex and replicated patterns.

In practice, observation and feedback are extremely important. By accepting that your organization exhibits patterns of actions and behaviors akin to a natural system, and then purposefully observing and making sense of these patterns, leaders and managers are provided with the information necessary to guide the work, collect feedback, and make informed adjustments. Feedback loops can be both positive and negative, neither particularly stable nor unstable, with these two contradictory sources pulling the system in opposite directions. Often referred to as "chaordic," a combination of chaos and order, feedback becomes a part of the basis for subsequent iterations of the pattern. It is these feedback loops, and the observation of how they change, that signals the leaders of changes ahead and where any adjustments need to be made (Cutright 2001; Gleick 1987; Tetenbaum 1998).

There is some good news in all of this: 1) problems and solutions often arise at the same time (Duggan 2007) and 2) several dimensions of self-organization suggest that a system often stays within a set of boundaries or patterns. The existence of *attractors* in an organization, described by Cutright as the elements (or people) within a system that draw organizational power, are where leaders need to invest and support in order to maintain structure and stability (Cutright 2001). In social settings like organizations, multiple attractors are often present in a system and act upon one another, with their interactions resulting in both an unstable and yet complex system of boundaries that constantly re-create and return to order.

Chaotic systems also display dimensions of self-similarity; that is, a pattern of the whole may be seen in any of its parts. These self-similarity patterns mimic those naturally occurring in systems like clouds, plants, and human biological systems and, like muscle memory, become increasingly familiar as the observer experiences the patterns on multiple occasions over an extended period of time.

When the principles of chaos theory are applied within an organization, and the organization is subjected to a dynamic and changing environment, the result is a feedback loop or loops composed of many complex interactions returned to the system, immediately modifying the organization's behavior. As a result, these dynamic feedback loops are effective for limited periods of time, awaiting the next inflow of information and feedback (Cutright 2001). As Scott (2008) suggests, "things happen around an organization that cannot be foreseen." In order to manage in these complex environments, leaders need to identify the centers of information flow, the attractors, and support them in their work. This is where the designed org structure, as depicted on the org chart, and the actual information and activities meet.

Complex Adaptive Systems (CAS)

Complex Adaptive Systems (CAS) theory crosses many traditional disciplinary boundaries. It is distinguished by its reliance on computer simulations as a research tool and places significant emphasis on systems such as markets or ecologies, which are less organized than those studied by more traditional approaches. Underlying the CAS theory are the many natural systems (e.g., beehives, snowflakes, and tree fronds) and, increasingly, many artificial ones (e.g., computing systems and artificial intelligence) characterized by increasingly complex behaviors, which emerge as a result of nonlinear interaction at different levels among naturally occurring biosystems and within organizations. These systems are known as Complex Adaptive Systems, dynamic systems that adapt to and evolve with a changing environment. Typically, in a CAS, there is no single centralized point of control that governs system behavior, and the system itself is much more than the sum of its parts. Similar to the attractors in the chaos system descriptions above, systems often self-organize with communication flowing to and through the individuals able to add the most value to the rest of the system's members, with mandates and rules having little to no practical value.

In a CAS, decisions or actions by one part of the system will influence all other related parts but not in a uniform or predictable manner. Very small changes can have a surprisingly profound impact on overall behavior, and in some cases, significant changes will have no effect. Executive management has little to no control over who shares what information with whom. As a result, these real systems are fundamentally unpredictable, and if ignored, can be, for most intents and purposes, impossible to control.

Complexity Leadership Theory (CLT)

Planning and management are difficult in times of disruptive change. Leaders need to be able to think ahead, evaluate the environment quickly, and then lead strategically. Planners need to forget the five- to ten-year time horizons and instead think in terms of six to twelve months and one to two years. As a result of the short timeframes for strategic plans, planning activities cannot be episodic events undertaken on some prescribed time increment but need to be approached with continuousness, frequency, and agility. In fact, organizations need to develop a top-down and bottom-up approach to strategy that will become part of a *culture of strategic thinking*.

Complexity Leadership Theory (CLT) is well suited to dynamic situations as goals are systematically evaluated and rapidly adjusted, and expertise comes and goes as projects necessitate. Leaders connect very deeply to frontline managers and staff in order to better understand the opportunities ahead, more strategically allocate resources, and then step back and let staff get work done. This complex or Agile model of planning and managing is not "out of control," as some uninformed critics might suggest, but rather has been well-studied with its roots in three types of complexity theory: *Leadership Complexity Theory*, *Dynamic Enterprise Theory*, and *Strategic Dynamism*. In all three theories, the fundamental hallmarks are creativity, adaptability, and innovation. Great organizations understand, embrace, and manage these ideas.

All of us leaders have, as part of our responsibilities, strategic planning. In my case, as I thought about how to proceed with planning, and then at what intervals to review and adjust the plan, I looked to traditional approaches that emphasize ways to inspire, motivate, and align subordinates around my goals and realized that these leader-driven approaches are becoming increasingly obsolete. I needed something fresh and new, an approach that recognized a modern world of growing complexity, interdependence, and interconnectivity where leaders moved away from hierarchy and control and toward building an understanding of how to manage increasing levels of complexity. For these newer approaches, I found it helpful to look to academic research and practitioner examples to help me decide what to do. Here are a few examples of approaches and studies that helped me develop and shape my own thinking about planning.

Although complexity is increasing and should result in responses that enable adaptive or complex dynamics, instead, many leaders answer with an ordered, top-down response that suppresses creativity and tamps down employee ambition and interest in leading. These approaches are often applied under the false illusion of control and predictability. Scholars attribute this phenomenon to the proliferation of leadership language and professional development activities that are designed for a bureaucratic rather than a complex context. Recently, Mary Uhl-Bien, a leadership scholar from the University of Nebraska, framed it simply: "It takes complexity to beat complexity" (Uhl-Bien 2007).

What this means to those of us trying to manage our organizations is that although complexity is increasing and should result in approaches that are adaptive and emergent in nature, many leaders instead answer with an ordered, top-down response that suppresses flexible and participative leadership. Uhl-Bien attributes this conflicted phenomenon to the proliferation of leadership messages and activities that are designed more for a bureaucratic rather than a complex context. Since innovation is one of the foundations of complex organizations, leaders need to focus on creating environments that foster creativity and encourage dissonance. Creating new knowledge should be a guiding principle as teams and strategies are developed. When leaders create environments designed to understand situations and contexts and link these with innovative and creative teams, organizations evolve and grow.

I always worked hard at staying informed, up to date, and well-practiced. So, as I began to plan for my newly launched business and started my executive roles in higher ed, I was surprised to find that planning seemed to be an isolated activity with little connection to strategy. This didn't make much sense then, nor does it make sense now. For those of us building organizations and running businesses, it is important to remember that for many management scholars, strategy "isn't planning; it is the intentional, informed, and integrated set of choices" made by a firm to direct its activities (Hambrick and Fredrickson 2001). It is the activity of planning that matters, not the plan.

It made a lot more sense to me to consider strategy, both planning and management, as an ongoing process of making strategic choices, often within a rapidly changing set of environmental conditions and competitive pressures that follow a circular path of moving from planning to management and back again—similar to the process of strategic flexibility and strategic dynamism referred to in scholarly literature. Scholars and practitioners widely accept that strategic planning flexibility and strategic dynamism are well-suited for those organizations facing complex and uncertain markets. Frankly, aren't we all facing rapid change and constant uncertainty? Since strategic dynamism is based on the relationship between an organization's capacity to rapidly respond to change and those responses that have a meaningful impact on a firm's performance, it makes sense to pay attention to the details of this approach. Strategically flexible firms quickly adjust their strategic plans and their strategic management practices to exploit market opportunities when they arise and to monitor and control the effect of environmental and competitive fluctuations on their performance.

Significant new research is underway to further explore the relationship between flexibility and firm performance, but generally, it is widely believed that in order to survive and prosper in turbulent and unpredictable environments, firms need to embrace strategic flexibility. Those firms able to quickly adjust their strategic plans in order to exploit market opportunities are likely to benefit by experiencing continuous improvements in customer value and achieving sustainable competitive advantage (Dibrell et al. 2007; Matthyssens et al. 2005). Let's briefly dig into strategic dynamism to learn what this is and how organizations might deploy its principles.

Strategic Dynamism

As an organizational leader, looking to scholarly writing related to the dynamic nature of strategy and performance and managing complex environments makes good sense. You will find that the dynamic capabilities referred to in strategic dynamism research are grounded in systems dynamics theory that suggests the interdependence between components as key to managing effectively. Strategy is, in practice, a dynamic and interactive process with three process-related components: Sensing, Seizing, and Reconfiguring. *Sensing* entails the continuous scanning of the external environment; *seizing* is characterized by an internal evaluation of resources and capabilities; *reconfiguring* entails the recombing of a firm's resources and capabilities to optimize internal capabilities with the environment (Markides 2008; Teece 2012). Studies show two important findings: 1) There is variation in the way firms accumulate and share knowledge, and 2) there is a positive relationship between dynamic capabilities and competitive advantage in dynamic environments. So, if you work in a dynamic industry and market, and most of us do, then this is an important management concept to consider.

Finally, it should also be of interest to know there is a relationship between resources and performance: Dynamic capabilities in high-velocity firms with resources outperform those where resources are scarce (Fainshmidt et al. 2019). Leaders need to consider how the dynamic nature of contemporary organizations, and dynamism in general, affects the way strategy is implemented and that a firm's dynamic capabilities and the availability of resources enables continuous and effective strategic shifting, allowing the firm to weather the storms of environmental, market, and competitive turbulence (Wilden, Devinney, and Dowling 2016). Dynamism creates "organizational dexterity" that has taken several firms like Amazon, IBM, and Toyota along paths to competitive advantage (O'Reilly and Tushman 2008). Context matters. Planning sets the stage for the direction of the firm and functions as the starting point for strategic dynamism, all aimed at gaining a competitive advantage. Here's another frame to consider when thinking about your organization.

Unified Structured Inventive Thinking

Unified Structured Inventive Thinking (USIT) is a structured, problem-solving methodology for finding innovative solutions to engineering-design type problems. Related to Systematic Inventive Thinking, USIT is a simple method that is quick to learn and easy to apply, requiring no database or system to manage. Originally called Structured Inventive Thinking and developed in a Ford Motor Company research lab, the methodology was modified and brought into Ford in the early 1990s. The goal of USIT is to enable teams working on problems to suggest multiple solutions in as short a time as possible, establish multiple and variable solutions, and then generate creative and logical solutions (Sickafus 2001).

For those of us without the resources or industry muscle that a company like Ford has, it is important to know that, in its earliest form, USIT featured "brainstorming" as the idea-generating, problem-solving process and suggested that early solutions, or "low-hanging fruit," were often the output and that this process can be effective with very few people and low levels of funding committed to driving it. Similar to scenarios in planning, the process then filtered the solutions or low-hanging fruit through a business and engineering team tasked with evaluating its financial and practical value and usefulness. In some cases, members of teams analyze whether the output from a particular analysis they have created is correct and then how they can prove their findings. Similar to Mike Rea's approach to teamwork and ideation, there are no right or wrong answers, only insights and degrees of effectiveness, and possibility and potential (Rea 2020). Sick-afus (2001) compares the process to "something like mathematics. When given a mathematics problem to work on, you don't need the answer. Using mathematical reasoning, you can test your solution's validity for yourself."

One key activity in the USIT process is the value of feedback. While that process refers to feedback in the context of electric circuits, it is worth considering how those feedback loops help explain the importance of that information flow for managers. In the USIT feedback description, there are several important features of problem-solving, all of which relate to organization and management:

1. The input or the problem under consideration can derive from any level of the problem definition (original problem statement > unwanted effect > objects, attributes, and functions > metaphors).
2. The team's past experiences change dynamically during the problem-solving process.
3. Two options exist for feedback: one is a modified trial/pilot, and the other is a modification of the problem.
4. The speed of the feedback should be accounted for and monitored.

In this approach, teams work within a loose structure to organize the ideation process and allow for testing and feedback, informing future iterations, pilots, and betas. How does this help the typical leader? What is clear is that by separating the ideation and evaluation processes, USIT provides room for the problem solvers to freely consider options and not get bogged down in the valuation and portfolio implications of their conclusions. For planners, it is critical to consider all scenarios and possibilities before analyzing the financial and portfolio implications. It is a mistake to allow constraints to stifle creativity and truncate possibilities. I like this problem-solving framework because, when combined with purposeful and systematic feedback, it can be brought together and included as a guiding principle in the new, Agile, asymmetrical, team-based ideation and problem-solving approach to management described in a later chapter. Now that we've identified ways to approach strategy in an increasingly complex context, we'll look at what organizational design is best equipped to handle this dynamic environment.

Chapter 10

ORGANIZATIONAL STRUCTURE AND STRATEGY

Along with knowing the benefits of the internal and external assessment tools at our disposal, we need to consider organizational structure. The structure of an organization can have a significant impact on how it operates. For example, financial services firms like banks need to have tightly structured processes and control systems, while design firms can operate more like free agencies with more fluid workflows.

An organization also has a "life" to consider. Meaning, it will develop over time, and different needs will arise along the way. The way things are structured in its early days is very likely to change as it evolves.

Where a firm falls on the maturation, size, and growth scales can also affect organization structure, with start-ups often lacking much, if any, structure and longer-lasting, more stable firms becoming increasingly bureaucratic over time. Successful organizations shift and adjust as they grow, matching structure with dynamic internal and external elements. In this context, one size does not fit all. In the book *The Structuring of Organizations*, Mintzberg describes organization structure as an interplay of strategy, environmental forces, and the structure in and of itself (Mintzberg

1979). When these forces fit well together, the organization performs well, and when they don't, it can generate significant problems.

To help you get a vision for where you are now structure-wise, let's look at some models.

Organizational Models

As many management scholars have described, organizations are comprised of formal and informal elements. While the formal elements often act as the blueprint for behavior, the informal ones actually influence what happens among the organization's members. Since there are myriad informal systems and relationships that are essential if an organization is to function with reasonable effectiveness, understanding how these processes work and turning them toward some collective goals is a distinct reality that leaders and planners must understand. The challenge is to strike a balance between the bureaucratic forms of organizing and the informal world of internal networks and connections. Based on this complex reality, leaders need to understand some of the basic theories at work in order to design a well-functioning organization.

According to Hall and Tolbert (2005), there are four organizational models: 1) population-ecology, 2) resource-dependence, 3) rational-contingency, and 4) institutional. The unique characteristics of each of the four models loosely correspond to those of the linear, hybrid, and chaos strategic planning models mentioned earlier in the book. For example, the actions taken by an organization may be the result of rigid planning (linear), or structures and symbols (hybrid), or highly changeable environmental factors (chaos), with the four organizational models providing a framework linking the organization's characteristics to its core values and culture. This linkage between strategic planning models and organizational structure allows management to match the environment, core capability, and structure with size, environment, and complexity.

The *population-ecology model* describes the organization as able to adapt to certain environmental conditions in much the same way as a biological system. Some organizations adapt to conditions better than others, and only the most adaptive survive. This model also emphasizes the organic nature of how an organization works, de-emphasizing the role of strategy and strategic choice in its structure, direction, and effectiveness. Criticism of the population-ecology model suggests sociality, power, capability, and competency play the lead role in organizational structure.

The *resource-dependence model* posits that the interpretation of environmental conditions and decisions are made by individual actors within the internal political context of organizations. Organizations following this model assume they cannot generate all the resources needed but must consider environmental forces when making strategic decisions and look to the environment in order to become self-sustaining. Internal power is critical in making choices, with organizational goals not the primary focus of the decision-making process. Compared to the population-ecology model, this model considers how structure is able to adapt to the environment rather than having the environment force an appropriate organizational form.

The *rational-contingency model* is a goals-based approach that acknowledges organizations have reasons for the things they do and that goals are part of the culture and the focus for decision-making. Organizations attempt to attain goals and deal with their environments, accepting that there are multiple ways to reach the same goals. In this model, prioritization of goals can be a source of competition among constituencies with measures of effectiveness up for interpretation and negotiation.

The *institutional model* notes that organizations are increasingly homogeneous—that is, they mimic or model each other. This perspective views organizational design as one that accepts internal and external pressures to conform to the others in an industry. In this model, the organization looks to others in their industry to imitate. It creates myths that become fact without regard for changing strategic realities. Real issues such as performance goals and efficiencies are downplayed, and ideas and practices come and go for no apparent reason.

As you move toward optimizing your organization's structure and strategy to handle current market and competitive pressures, another factor has to be considered that is beyond structure: complexity.

Complex Organizations

In the early twentieth century, organizations were often large bureaucracies, managed from the top down with the executive suite populated by the founder and his relatives. Decision-making was centered at the very top, with little to no input from line managers and workers. Planning was virtually nonexistent, wages were low, adequately skilled labor was in plentiful supply, and discipline and subservience were expected from employees (Scott 2008). As industrialization progressed, workers began to feel a sense of empowerment, and they could, to a certain degree, share in the bounties of success (Perrow 1986). Much of the research in institutional theory during this period was based on political systems, language, and legal systems, mostly ignoring organizational form and symmetry and innovation. The scientific management movement also emerged during this period with three primary tenets:

1. Research was applied to worker productivity (in the form of time study);
2. By applying this research to work, management could assign tasks to employees based on their skills; and
3. Cooperation between management and labor was assumed.

Applying these principles to labor resulted in increased specialization (and profits), the need for a different kind of management structure to oversee these growing mechanized organizations, and the birth of the modern bureaucracy.

It wasn't until the mid-1970s and 1980s that the significance of the organization's structure and how it affected planning, operations, and performance was recognized and studied (Hall and Tolbert 2005; Perrow

1986; Scott 1992 and 2008). According to Perrow (1986) and consistent with Weber's model of bureaucracy (2003), nearly all large, complex organizations in the United States were bureaucracies—including colleges and universities. These bureaucracies were identified by characteristics that include universalistic standards or tenure for employees, a systematic division of labor, workers' rights, tension related to the control and use of power, official rules and goals, and impersonality.

Bureaucracy

Management scholars generally accept that higher education is an example of the professional bureaucracy or professional organization (Bolman and Deal 2008; Mintzberg 1989; Raines and Leathers 2003; Scott 2008; Wilms and Zell 2002). A professional organization's structure is largely built upon a group of individual professionals working within the controls of their discipline, with much of the decision-making by collective choice. The overall strategy is often fragmented, unstable, and subject to continual change—conditions that lead to dependence on the central administration for resources, what Mintzberg (1989) referred to as "forced cohesion." In many loosely coupled organizations like higher education, departments tend to be autonomous and follow the strategies determined by the department's administration, often with little regard for, or connection to, central administration (Wilms and Zell 2002). This decentralized structure allows the professionals to gain collective control over those decisions that affect them by maintaining seats on influential committees and organizing collective support for initiatives (Jones 2001; Mintzberg 1989).

In practice, two structures emerge: one bottom-up, with professionals driving decisions up to administrators, and the other with administrators at the top, driving decisions down to the staff. Power in these organizations is often found with those individuals who can locate resources (and have a say in how they are distributed), shield professionals from the bureaucracy, and are otherwise perceived as serving the interests of the professionals (Mintzberg 1989).

Mintzberg wrote extensively about organizational structure and its impact on strategy. In his classic five types of organizational structures work, he categorized these types by structural form, application, and risks. While a detailed discussion about Mintzberg may not be needed, at this point, some mention of the structures and their highlights is called for in order to understand the interplay between structure and strategy:

1. **Entrepreneurial Organization:** Simple and flat in design, these organizations are relatively unstructured and informal compared to other forms. Example: Start-ups.
2. **Machine Organization:** More standardized and formal, these organizations consist of functional groups with tight, vertical structure. Example: Universities.
3. **Professional Organization:** Bureaucratic, these organizations consist of highly trained professionals who control most of their own work. Example: Consulting companies.
4. **Diversified Organization:** An organization with many different product lines and businesses often consisting of a central office with dispersed satellites. Example: Multinational banks.
5. **Innovative Organization:** Companies consisting of project teams with decentralized power and decision-making. Control is a significant challenge. Example: Pharmaceuticals.

Mintzberg's classification is just one way to consider how structure and strategy relate. There is no prescription or "right way" to structure an organization. What we do know is that the attributes uncovered during the SWOT process (e.g., the organization's strengths, weaknesses, opportunities, and threats) should be complemented by the structure and that the speed of work and the pressure to adapt are creating new hybrid forms of organizations of all shapes and sizes in all industries. In a recent article by McKinsey & Company, they suggest that "amid the fear and uncertainty, people are energized as companies make good on purpose statements, eliminate bureaucracy, empower previously untested leaders with big respon-sibilities, and 'turbocharge' decision making," indicating the need for flat structures, thin hierarchies, and applying an Agile approach to managing (D'Auria et al. 2020).

PART 4:

Managing the Pivot

Chapter 11

A NATURAL EVOLUTION: TRADITIONAL TO AGILE

"In a period of transition from a deliberate strategy
to an emergent one whose contours are not yet clear,
or vice versa, perhaps that is acceptable—even good.
In such cases, sometimes the best strategy is sustained
exploration, prototyping, trials, and pilot testing."
—Lindblom (1990); Mulgan (2009); Kay (2010)
and Otto Scharmer (2016)

Agile (adj. the ability to think quickly; mentally acute or aware)

As we know, leaders need new business models to adapt to an increasingly dynamic and rapidly changing world. They need to act quickly and remain on alert and aware of the environment in which they operate. Organizations have been beating up planners for years, and those of us who believe in planning, and pushing for plans, have been yelled at, ignored, and shouted out of conference rooms. Yet, despite all this disagreement and stress, it is clear that something's not working in strategy land. Organizations were caught off-guard in 2008 when the stock market corrected, and the Great Recession hit. Businesses folded, universities contracted, and leaders reached for any available life raft to weather the storm, and now, in 2020, the cycle is repeating itself because of the pandemic.

Why do leaders allow their organizations to be susceptible to these cycles, and what can be done to prepare for the next one? For CEOs who live quarter to quarter, if the next set of financial reports aren't negatively affected, there's no reason to care. However, for the rest of us, the time seems right to consider new ways of doing business, new ways to plan, new ways to match competencies with opportunities, new ways to allocate resources that are more strategic and less idiosyncratic, and new ways to thrive in an increasingly dizzying state of dynamism.

Organizations, regardless of industry, will need to reduce the time between idea generation and execution, provide the guideposts but not a hard direction for smart teams to ideate, embed innovation and ideation and creativity into their cultures, and design and manage organizational structures that allow for observation, analyses, and quick reaction—preparing to Pivot as ideas and insights uncover opportunities. Looking back at an earlier example, Unilever's story of getting hand sanitizer to market within six to seven weeks after the pandemic began was a strong step into the waters of Agile management. The urgency of the situation accelerated their commitment to becoming an end-to-end Agile company, driving them forward fast. "We had to capture insight fast and deliver value quickly" (Ferrazzi 2020). Before we get into Agile management in too much detail, let's take a quick look at the concept of Agility and what we've been doing that got us to where we are.

Agility (noun. the ability to move nimbly with speed and ease)

As you can see in this diagram, planning has evolved from a linear, lockstep activity, to a robust and continuous "plan, do, assess, and feedback" cycle:

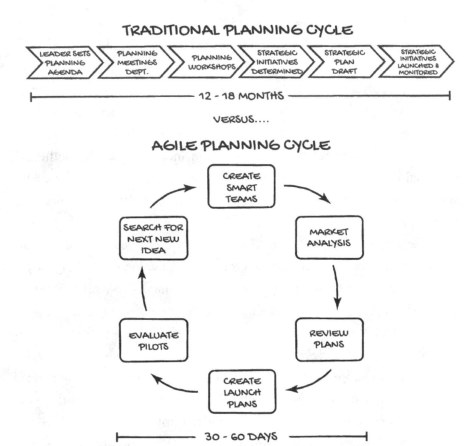

Organizations need to act quickly, with speed and nimbleness. In his recent book, *The Age of Agile*, Stephen Denning argues one of the three core characteristics of Agile organizations is the "Law of the Customer," meaning customer primacy needs to be at the center of all the company does. Companies need to partner with customers in an Agile and responsive way to solve problems and fulfill needs. Companies need to work directly with customers to determine the optimal mix of products and/or services, how to best reach existing and new markets, and how to provide continuous improvement of their offerings in order to attract and keep customers. Forget the twentieth-century notion of "inputs in and value-added out." Instead, the twenty-first-century perspective is about "partnering, collaboration, and iterative customer-centered delivery," what those in the IT and continuous improvement worlds refer to as "relentless Agility."

What happens to businesses if this message is ignored? The insidious nature of the current dynamic era of business is having an almost Darwinian effect on organizational effectiveness and successful performance, and they will be weeded out. As businesses operate at a continuously accelerated pace and complicated systems become increasingly commoditized, existential choices need to be made. Will the large organizations of the twentieth century continue to exist? Maybe, but unlikely in the same form as in the past.

For example, recently, Elon Musk, Tesla's CEO, announced the one million-mile EV battery for their electric cars, a development likely to disrupt car companies (and energy companies) around the world (Baldwin 2020). Which will survive? Will there be concentration and consolidation in the industry? Will new companies have the same opportunities to grow and thrive as existing ones? To all three questions, the answer is… maybe. What's likely to happen is that there will be fewer car companies surviving this disruption, and those that do will follow the meteoric rise of the technology titans of recent history (e.g., Google, Apple, Amazon, and Microsoft). Those companies, having the capital, expertise, and *operating agility* to seize the opportunities, will thrive, and the rest, clinging to the technologies and methodologies of the past, will fade away.

For existing organizations, whether they are looking to enter new markets or extend an advantage, you are one unplanned event or pandemic or economic downturn or climate crisis away from survival. The stakes have never been higher. The need for speed and agility never greater.

The Bigger Picture

In one lifetime, many of us have gone from a pocket calculator and spiral notebook to a powerful cell phone and laptop computer, used to take notes in school or at work, each effective, each having very different capabilities and usefulness. These seismic shifts in how we do work are driving profound changes in the approach to planning and strategy due to the exponential changes in technology, globalization, competition, and communications. In this era of rapid change, a whole new approach to work needs to be developed, an approach that applies across businesses, institutions, nonprofits, and the government.

In order to understand where we are now, I believe it's important to take a look back and briefly review the evolution of strategic management theory, beginning at the turn of the twentieth century and leading up to the beginning of the twenty-first century. Starting with Frederick Taylor and Henry Fayol at the end of the nineteenth and beginning of the twentieth centuries, Henry Markowitz and Warren Bennis in the early-to the mid-century and late twentieth century, early twenty-first-century strategists including Clayton Christensen, Peter Drucker, Henry Mintzberg, Tom Peters, and Michael Porter—the study of strategic management has become increasingly sophisticated as industries evolved and scholarship matured.

Why look back? Because we need to recognize beliefs and attitudes that have been promoted for many decades and are still predominant, which can help or hinder us in moving ahead.

Beyond that look back, we'll look ahead, offering you better options for strategic planning and management—not just a static, one-time effort but on an ongoing basis.

The goal is to help you learn about and implement a better way to plan than past organizations have relied on. Using Agile techniques from project management theory, Agile organizations—led by smart, well-trained individuals highly aware of market forces—are created that could significantly alter their approach to planning and strategic management. So, what does the organization need to do? Steve Denning's table comparing Agile management and twentieth-century management practices is a good summary of how management has changed as a result of applying Agile principles (e.g., moving from horizontal levels of competence vs. vertical hierarchies, leadership at every valley vs. leadership by title, and attracting and retaining strong talent vs. hiring and controlling people and positions [Denning, 2020]).

Another useful way to consider comparing traditional and Agile approaches can be found in Darrell Rigby's "Agile Operating Model." In that approach, organizations avoid the illusion of easy wins and, instead, go for preparation, team readiness, close collaboration with customers, rapid prototyping, and fast feedback loops. By breaking down large, complex projects into smaller parts and then launching small Agile teams to design and test solutions for each part, Agile methods are used to accelerate the work and solve problems. Important aspects of ramping up Agile include recruiting star players, incentivizing team rather than individual successes, and assigning joint accountability to ensure focus at the team level (Rigby, Sutherland, and Noble 2018). Agile follows a core principle of "test and learn" that is incremental and iterative in nature but innovative and expansive in outcomes.

A terrific example of using scenarios as a tool in the planning toolbox can be found at the Shell Oil Corporation's smart scenario planning program that began in the 1970s and is still in use today. While scenarios will be discussed in more detail later, it is useful to know that scenario planning has never been more important as institutions and organizations consider many different potential future situations for which they need to be prepared. Smart scenario planning may be converted into algorithms that can be managed by computer programs. They can help improve our understanding of the interrelationship between future potential events and the effect(s) on output and performance (e.g., finances, production, service providing, and shareholder/stakeholder value). Using scenarios is but one way to evolve and improve strategic planning. Now, how do you apply it to your organization?

Evolving Traditional Planning to Agile

Traditional planning often begins by answering several questions related to projects and programs at the earliest conceptual stage. Where do we start?

What needs to be built? When does it need to be completed? How much will it cost? Who are the stakeholders? Are there any competitors or similar products or services in the marketplace? Working with owner/funders, the task of the project manager is to manage and document a process that answers the above questions and follows a regimented process that looks something like this:

1. Establish objectives.
2. Develop requirements.
3. Define the scope of work.
4. Identify activities and dependencies.
5. Estimate the level of effort, including timelines and budgets.
6. Receive owner approval.

Once the scope of work is determined (e.g., build a building, develop a software application, or fabricate a new jet fighter), the project manager determines the tasks or activities required to complete the scope of work and accomplish the goals. Then, as referred to in #4 above, the project manager identifies the relationship between activities or dependencies since these activities rely on (or depend on) the work of another preceding activity (e.g., foundations are built first, walls second—dependent on the foundations being completed, and then third, the roof—dependent on the walls being completed). By developing a plan of the activities in list form and then determining dependencies, the project manager can build a logic diagram or plan. Projects with large quantities of individual parts, as in a new building project with millions of individual components, or a software development project with millions of lines of interdependent code, or a jet fighter with millions of specially designed parts, projects become extremely complex very quickly, requiring sophisticated software like MS Project, Smartsheet, or CoConstruct to manage the parts, dependencies, and progress. Once the logic is determined, it's time to get started. This is where Agile planning and Agile management come together. First, let's dig a little deeper into Agile planning.

Now that you know how to create strategic plans that are designed to respond to an increasing level of complexity and industry disruption, let's take a look at how those plans are used as guides by managers and management and how they are adjusted, implemented, and improved.

Regardless of type, industry, and size, organizations are finding that following Agile principles makes their strategic planning processes more iterative, responsive, and flexible. Why bother creating plans that are unresponsive to industry conditions? The principle that undergirds planning is to utilize the organization's competencies and expertise to address the needs of the customer(s) and as a guide for its future activities. When Agile planning principles are applied to strategic initiatives and activities, performance measures are linked tightly to the short- and mid-term vision, with the likelihood of increased success. Agile provides the framework for continuous planning that, as part of a team approach, allows for the continuous evaluation of performance and adjustments to goals as experience and conditions dictate. Flexibility and responsiveness are operating principles—concepts and terminology not normally related to planning.

Agile planning can be broken down into seven activities.

1. **Start with a big picture**. Whether it's a house, commercial building, or software project, you need to define the vision for the project and describe the themes that connect to the organization's strategy. What should we be focusing on over the next six or twelve months? Where do we want to spend our time and resources? What specific activities do we want to accomplish, and on what timeline? And then finally, who is responsible?

2. **Link initiatives to resources or the strategic and financial plans**. Are we stable and able to invest in new strategies? Where will cap-

ital or venture capital come from? Who do we need "in the know" to help secure the resources needed?

3. **Divide operating and strategic initiatives into manageable chunks.** By breaking down complexity into more granular pieces, it gives the leadership team and the managers a clearer line of sight into the operation, the new initiatives, and the organization's goals. In the spirit of "what isn't measured isn't managed," this is the time to load the plan into a software program so that it is refined. Iterations can then be communicated to stakeholders and saved for future reference.

4. **Create cost and time estimates for the initiatives and activities in the plan.** By creating a vision in the earliest steps and then attaching cost and time estimates, it really creates a clear and understandable path forward. As the fiscal year or period begins, a continuous review of the activities, the costs, and the timeline are part of the day-to-day executive team discussions in order to keep the P&L and new initiatives on track.

5. **Divide large, complex initiatives, activities, or goals into smaller, more granular parts,** including costs and timelines for each, to ensure your increasingly Agile leadership team is able to measure progress on a weekly, monthly, and quarterly basis. This Agile-inspired approach maintains enthusiasm and focus.

6. **Connect the plan to the organization's mission, vision, and core values.** Once the organization's plan is developed and the details completed as described in earlier steps, create communication devices in order to share the plan throughout the organization and with key customers. Remember, a strategy not shared is a strategy not delivered.

7. **Build a culture of continuous planning and continuous improvement.** No plan is ever really complete as internal and external conditions continuously change. So, continuing to deliver value

through these incremental improvements really aligns the work of the organization with current and future plans.

It is important to remember that Agile is not a strategy. It is a capability and an approach to managing. A strategy is not a plan but a decision-making framework or a set of guiding principles that can be applied as situations evolve and opportunities emerge (Bungay 2019).

Since one of the core principles of Agile is the inclusion of your customer(s) in all that you do, it makes sense to include them in the creation of your organization's strategic plan. By taking this powerful and affirmative step, your organization builds confidence in the relationship by putting the needs of the customer front and center and demonstrating that their needs are squarely at the forefront of your organization's plans. While it's not a traditional approach, the customer's input and participation make the plan better and more relevant. As described in the Agile Manifesto, focusing on "customer collaboration over contract negotiation" allows for the organization and its customer(s) to work out the details of the initiatives most valuable to the customer *and* how the organization is planning to fill the order or provide the service in the next six- to twelve-month period. Agile principles affirm that the closer you are to your customer, the better and, as a core value of the Agile, the successful twenty-first-century organization is, if nothing else, an arm of the customer responsible for building new products, provide services, solve problems, and create value.

Evolving Traditional Management to Agile

First, let's take a quick look at the process for managing complex projects. I've managed hundreds of construction and software projects and have found that the overwhelming challenge common to each is the management and coordination related to the many moving parts within three primary constraints: Scope, Budget, and Schedule, often referred to as the "Triple Constraints," or "Iron Triangle."

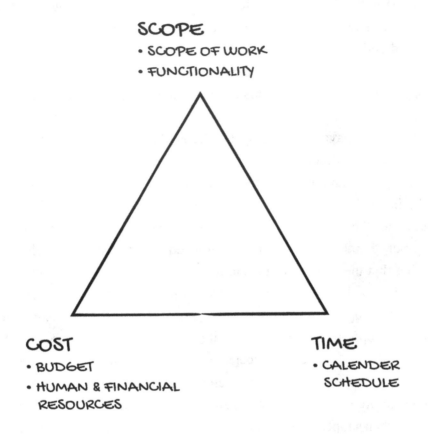

SCOPE
- SCOPE OF WORK
- FUNCTIONALITY

COST
- BUDGET
- HUMAN & FINANCIAL RESOURCES

TIME
- CALENDER SCHEDULE

These three elements of projects are interdependent, that is, when one of these elements is restricted or extended (more or less scope, higher or lower budget, longer or shorter timeline), the other two elements will then also need to be either extended/increased or restricted/reduced in some way. For example, in a recent software project, the owner asked for more functionality (scope), and when he did, the project manager said that there would an increase in the timeline (schedule) and cost (budget). Balancing all three elements is key to managing a project successfully and the primary responsibility of the project manager.

Of course, balancing the three elements sounds easier in theory than practice, and while project managers try to balance all three, experience agrees with what a chief technology officer friend once told me, "Gerry, you can have two, but not all three." Once a project leaves the drawing board and a timeline and overall plan are determined, the next headache for the project manager is managing the project in the field, and things begin to change. Snowstorms and tornadoes happen, owners change their minds, and mistakes are commonplace by the designers, engineers, and architects. I have lived through hundreds of these situations in many building and IT projects.

In the traditional or waterfall method of project management, when the inevitable changes occur, the project manager is responsible for calculating the additional costs and time and obtaining the approval of the owner or authorized party before proceeding, often creating delays. Realizing that the relative scope and impact of these individual changes were usually small and that, historically, projects would go over the baseline budget by up to 10% for my projects, I would request not-to-exceed authorization upfront for both individual ($x) and total change order costs ($y, up to $z total) in order to accelerate the change and approval process and keep the project on track. In essence, the cost to delay the project while change orders were calculated, and in many cases negotiated, was much more than simply allowing the project manager to keep the project moving and be responsible for managing to an agreed-upon total.

Despite what software aficionados might say, Agile was in full swing in the construction industry in the 1990s. Referred to as "fast track," construction management firms were specializing in this method, and, in fact, in my career as a project manager, I managed most of my projects using this approach. The Agile Manifesto, originally published by a small group of software engineers in 2001, was a new approach to software development that addressed the constant delays present in following traditional and waterfall methods. Highlighting twelve key principles, project managers in other industries, including this book's author and other project managers in real estate development and construction, realized that this approach could work in their situations as well. In the 2000s, most software and construction projects and project managers used some or most of the Agile principles. Increasingly, Agile is being applied to the management and success of many businesses (Denning 2020c).

> *"In the Merriam-Webster dictionary, agile means marked by*
> *ready ability to move with quick, easy grace and having*
> *a quick resourceful and adaptable character."*
> —Joshua Kerievsky

A primary difference between Agile management and the traditional project management approach lies in the relationship between the contractor/developer and the customer. As described previously, in traditional project management, activities proceed one step at a time in a serial manner, with many interdependencies. Before the project team can move forward in any specific phase or with any changes, the owner needs to be brought up to speed and approve any changes, which slows down progress, often compromising the final product. In Agile or fast track, the customer works side-by-side with the planning team as their goals and ideas are relied upon for conceptual designs that translate into specifications, plans, scopes of work, budgets, and timelines. These "plans and specs" are visual expressions of the customer's vision for the project and will, in addition to the "I really want the building to look like this" or "I really want the software to operate like that," include the scope, cost, and schedule for the work (the "Triple Constraints").

In my experience, the resistance to using fast track or Agile approaches to projects of any sort usually lies in an owner's lack of understanding of the process and the perceived loss of leverage between them and the contractor/developer. In traditional approaches, designers create a design, and owners negotiate with contractors or developers on a lump sum basis. Owners assume because they have leverage, they are likely to get the best deal. In fact, projects are a collection of labor and materials that constantly change due to material availability, obsolescence, labor disputes, material sourcing issues, acts of God, etc. As a result, the plans and specs are being continually interpreted and adjusted along the way and where misunderstanding and distrust enter the project picture.

In an Agile approach, much of the adversarial dynamics between contractor and customer are eliminated since the customer is part of the team. Project teams can eliminate many of the traditional cost disagreements by estimating labor and materials on an open book basis. This open book or Agile approach provides the owner with assurances that there is both transparency and control of project costs, allowing the process to move forward with owner consent in an iterative and cooperative manner. By starting the work immediately after the concept phase is complete and then working with the owner to iterate and test some of the underlying project assumptions, this savings of time provides both the contractor/developer and the owner with the ability to adjust the scope budget and schedule in a way that meets both party's goals—and allows the team to get to work. Let's get into more detail in the next chapter.

Chapter 12

AGILE: FILLING A GAP IN MANAGEMENT

"Agility: It rhymes with stability."
—McKinsey & Company

Now That We Have All These Cool Ideas, What Do We Do?

When comparing planning and managing, the former is like playing chess where the players have perfect information to work with (thus, they can plan), and the latter like playing poker where the players have little information but still have to play (managing). If strategy is about gaining a competitive advantage, then leaders and managers must learn to play poker.

As mentioned earlier, Agile is becoming an increasingly familiar approach to the management of organizations in industries of all sorts, an approach designed to cope with continuous and unrelenting change. It is the best way to manage the information flow and ideation resulting from an asymmetric planning process that, by its very nature, produces lots of ideas and insights that need evaluation, analysis, and consideration. In theory, building an enterprise consisting of Agile teams diligently working on problems and developing solutions should be easy. Right? The staff all want responsibility and accountability. To be the masters of their destiny. Right? Well, maybe not. While Agile principles have been in use in software development since around 2001 with good results, this project management approach has been used by relatively small teams working on specific projects. The application of Agile principles across an entire enterprise is a relatively new approach to strategic management that may present some challenges.

One example of deploying Agile principles at the enterprise level can be found in the software-based, smaller-team version of Agile, known in industry circles as the "Scaled Agile Framework" or SAFe. The SAFe framework, well known for its use at the project level, has recently been extended to the corporate setting with companies like Lego and Spotify using it with great success. Best described as a combination of Agile and lean project management, SAFe can be used to develop and test products faster and at a lower cost. Working in shorter cycles or smaller increments, SAFe uses the least amount of space, equipment, material, and staff resources to get things done. Imagine an organization with several teams working under their own version of an Agile framework, all following slightly different processes requiring specific tools and producing output in different forms. Since Agile teams tend to work bottom-up in the project-based organization structure, coordination becomes a real challenge. That bottom-up approach is simply not practical. While seemingly antithetical to Agile principles, following a more top-down approach locates direction-giving at the top (core and administrative functions) and decision-making with each team. It allows central administration to provide common tools and reporting that helps the system gain efficiency, consistency, and cross-functional practicality.

Critical to the effective use of SAFe is centralized decision-making that brings a sense of structure and strategy into the process that, along with standardized processes, creates better horizontal business alignment among R&D, product, and core operating departments (e.g., marketing, finance, HR, and IT). This gives teams a stake in the process, improves motivation, and increases productivity. By centralizing the strategy, standardizing tools, and maintaining core functions in the core, some dependency on central administration is created as information and communication is exchanged and connectivity encouraged. In practice, SAFe companies have improved R&D output, faster delivery times, and higher levels of employee satisfaction and could serve as a model for how product management works in Agile management (Agile Center 2020a).

In the Unilever example described earlier, Michael Clementi, the Executive Vice President of HR, says that "what's great about Agile is you're working on one project, the most important, highest value project, and teams are unified around the top priorities. There is no need for long, drawn-out meetings and conference calls. Everyone knows what to do and they just do it" (Ferrazzi 2020). He suggests there are three areas of emphasis to pay attention to if your organization wants to operate in an Agile way:

1. Emphasize the customer needs, not the process.
2. Emphasize prioritization like crazy.
3. Produce and share project briefs to ensure alignment and speed.

> *"Agile is a great way of adapting, of accelerating evolution.*
> *It protects and preserves the good parts of what's going on*
> *and changes the parts that need to adapt. It's at that*
> *golden mean between stasis and chaos."*
> —Darrell Rigby, Bain & Company

As we look to Agile as a model for a new approach to management, we realize that the best (only?) way to cope with the rapidly increasing velocity of information and communications—the global nature of every industry—is to create smart, self-organizing teams capable of working directly with customers to solve problems and add value. I think we can agree that the old order of things, highlighted by rigid structures and slow-moving bureaucracies, is no longer workable in the current dynamic, global, and competitive environment. How do we cope? If we believe an Agile approach is workable, how would that work?

As you may be able to tell by now, many of the most current examples of Agile management principles cited in this book are beginning to overlap. The similarities and any related ideas, concepts, or improvements will be aggregated and converted into an Agile management model that follows. At this point, by using an Agile management framework, organizations have core operating values, including teamwork, customer-centered planning and projects, the constant scanning of the environment for new knowledge and new opportunities, and then once opportunities emerge, the ability to quickly Pivot to avoid the next crisis or take advantage of opportunities. In this way, organizations are better able to cope with the constant change in their industry or market and avoid being blindsided by the next natural disaster. How companies move from ideation to action or idea to execution is the subject of the next few pages.

From Idea to Execution

> *"If there was any justice in the world,*
> *Agile would be awarded the Nobel Prize for management."*
> —Steve Denning

There were many times in my roles in both the corporate sector and higher education when I wondered whether the underperforming programs or projects I encountered, or in some cases adopted, were the result of poor strategy, poor execution, or something else. When facing underperformance in programs as far-flung as degree programs, executive education, certificates, research centers, or high-rise and medical renovation projects, it wasn't easy to identify the root cause of the poor results. Until recently, performance data—used to gauge progress at most organizations—were the lifeblood of my small company and other companies I consulted. Ironically, in higher education, these data were difficult to find and nearly impossible to aggregate into useful reports, and even more rarely, paid attention to. What did seem like a common problem was the lack of implementation expertise and commitment, the lack of interest in performance measurement, and the lack of accountability from top to bottom. In the last few years, by rolling out new, single-entry, activity-based accounting systems at both business schools, school leadership had the performance data in real time for the first time, whether they wanted it or not, and were forced to confront low- or non-performing programs. Dashboards provided real-time program and project performance. Deans, vice presidents, and executives could no longer ignore reality as the institution was dragged, in some cases kicking and screaming, into the twenty-first century.

In my experience, organizations enjoying consistent success spent some amount of time in formal strategic planning activities and some in managing the planning to execution handoff. Here are some implementation approaches and practices for you to consider.

In a recent PwC survey of over 700 executives across a wide swath of industries, their consultants found that only 8% of company leaders were said to excel at both strategy and execution and that "the days of keeping strategy and execution as separate topics are ending" (PwC 2017). Companies and executives agree that creating a continuous and strategic process, which includes planning, piloting, evaluating, and adjusting, needs to be part of the organization's DNA. What do you make of this? If these two capabilities seem difficult to master simultaneously, what's driving the need to integrate them? Are these really very different competencies? The answers are yes and yes.

In the past, it was common to put leaders into three buckets: visionaries and operators, planners and implementers, and thinkers and doers. Today, leaders need to be all three. They need to be able to build a compelling strategy, ensure the organization is investing in that vision, and then compel their stakeholders to take the journey to high performance and positive results. This is harder than it sounds and often begins with Agile teams planning and then managing and executing. What's so hard about this? Let's take a deeper look.

While Agile has recently become the de facto approach for software development, it has been slowly adopted for general management use. More often than not, executives trained by US business schools managed using hierarchy and structure to control, measure, and drive results. Agile teams came together to manage individual projects, most often without autonomy or accountability, delivering projects with mixed results. In fact, the Project Management Institute (PMI) reported in 2016 that projects were deemed successful approximately 60% of the time, up from less than 50% a decade ago (PMI 2018). Despite the trend showing that an Agile approach to managing is having increasingly positive results at the project level, when asked to deliver projects either by customers in the corporate setting or institutional leaders in higher ed, I have been told over and over that "I don't know anything about Agile" and "I don't care how you get it done, just get it done." Thus, when Agile is suggested as a management approach, it's no wonder these same leaders have little interest in learning how the approach works and how it can be used to manage their enterprises.

As an executive and member of a number of for-profit and nonprofit boards, I've often heard the cry "we need a strategic plan," as if that were the answer to whatever was ailing the organization. Rather than spending the time planning and then ignoring the plan, what would best serve the organization is a robust, dynamic, and responsive new approach to strategy—one grounded in the principles of Agile management. As a leader, you need both an Agile plan and an Agile strategy, and if you have a bad strategy or no strategy, know that excellent execution will not save you (Duggal 2018). Once the plan(s) is set, the handoff between the planners and the managers becomes critical to crisp execution.

For the purposes of Agile management, these two activities cannot be separated and, in fact, must come together "linking planning with agile execution" (Hadaya and Gagnon 2020). Wide-open transparency and the *continuous exchange* of performance data between the planners and project teams are the keys to tracking performance and feeding information back to the planners in order to guide the next new project. What I have found that works well is for each project and each team to prepare a brief business plan, perhaps not at the investor-level of detail, but a version where the project's purpose and level of resources needed are explained, along with a prepared market and costs analysis and an ROI against which to track progress. The team can then build it out in more detail as the project moves forward.

In the well-documented case of Starbucks, their strategy includes putting the interests of their employees front and center. As part of the culture, employees, referred to as "partners," operate in a relationship-driven, employee-first approach that encourages feedback and idea generation. They are consulted on things like store décor, music, and food selections. Howard Schultz, Starbucks' founder and chairman, has a unique combination of visionary and operator skills that have driven the company to sustainable success. Leaders able to master both competencies can 1) build an executable strategy, 2) take the time to educate the rest of the company in the vision and strategy, and 3) motivate the entire company to go on the journey (Leinwand and Rotering 2017).

One way to bridge the strategy-to-execution gap is to create Agile Roadmaps. Often used in software projects, these maps are readily adaptable for management's use as a guide for planning, from Agile to action, so progress can be made while you get the funding and support you need to move forward. Roadmaps allow you to plan initiatives in a fraction of the time and cost, and when coupled with scenarios and ideation, help planning teams consider all options, evaluate ROI, and deliver benefits much sooner at a lower cost (Robinson 2020).

I was recently introduced to the founder and CEO of a small and successful storage rack company specializing in the manufacture of surfboards, bicycles, and other accessories for "extreme sports" products. As his executive coach, I asked him in the earliest meetings how he and his team decided what items to sell and if they did any market research to estimate demand before spending the money to build prototypes. He told me that "we decide what's cool and then prototype it and list it on the website. We hope our customers find it, like it, and want to buy it." In the short run, while the company is small, this lack of a roadmap may be okay but in the words of a business school colleague: "Hope is not a strategy." So, my advice is to follow a logical process or roadmap by understanding potential market demand, design and prototype products, market test, and then invest in winners and disinvest in losers.

Successful organizations develop bold strategies that begin with understanding the organization's distinctive capabilities (What are we good at?), analyzing how far they can take the idea (What are we able to achieve?), and then empowering product teams to execute the work (What do you need to get going?). In this way, when an opportunity presents itself, teams are well-practiced and able to move quickly, seamlessly, and purposefully from vision to strategy to execution, with a sense of urgency and accountability for results. The days of inventing a cool product that is the brainchild of an inventive founder or offering a service the founder thinks is valuable, and then investing in the idea without clearly understanding the market and hoping for a positive outcome is an approach destined for failure.

The Strategy to Execution Gap

Recently, scholars and practitioners have been writing about the importance of managing the gap between strategy and execution, implying that these were two separate and distinct activities. Clearly, they should not be. Some organizations try to close the strategy to execution gap by constantly analyzing markets and looking for market opportunities (strategy focus), while others place bets on execution by improving methods and practices (Leinwand and Mainardi 2016). However, neither approach, in and of itself, is enough. In this information and knowledge age, leaders and managers need to be planning and executing as one process as fast as their organizational synapses can process. The challenge is to balance speed with process integration and communication to ensure the idea or program gets from idea to execution or from planning to implementation cleanly and clearly. Companies like Apple, Lego, Qualcomm, and Starbucks are well-known for high-speed idea generation and high-impact execution across multiple business lines, a capability that has, in and of itself, created a competitive advantage. By dynamically linking your strategy and execution and building distinctive capabilities, organizations are able to converge these distinctly separate activities into one, resulting in what we aspire for, to bring planning and strategy together as one, single stream of continuous work. So, how do you do this?

Leinwand and Mainardi (2016) suggest that the development of these five habits can lead to seamless execution:

1. Commit to an identity; differentiate and grow based on what you do best.
2. Translate the strategic into the everyday; build and develop cross-functional depth.
3. Put your culture to work; leverage your cultural strengths.
4. Cut costs to grow stronger; prune and invest in what matters.
5. Shape your future; reimagine your capabilities, create demand, and innovate.

In general, this five-habit framework is a simple and easy way to think about execution and can be found, in some form, in most contemporary strategy literature, often followed by research that supports the proposition that when companies develop these habits, competitive advantage is sure to follow. However, I'm not sure it's quite that easy, so let's keep digging in. From the very first kernel of a business idea to shaping and refining it, and then proposing it to leadership and getting the work approved, speed and creativity are always in demand. If you are launching a new company or project, or your organization wants to grow by broadening the portfolio or expanding into new markets, it is critical to follow this Agile principle: Listen to your customer, and once you agree on a new product or service and have identified and committed the necessary resources, energize your execution team and go, fast.

Who is responsible for closing the gap? Who leads the transition of a new product or initiative from plan to live project? Certainly, key organizational leaders, either because of their positions or their informal networks, and often not those in the executive suite, help close the strategy to execution gap. Staff, who are closest to the action and know a lot about the organization's core competencies and customer needs, are best equipped to bring the organization's skills together in unique ways and are the best equipped to connect their work to the overall strategy of the organization. Ironically, in a recent survey by PwC, only 28% of employees felt fully connected to the purpose and identity of their organization, negatively affecting their motivation and commitment, making staff development and staff support a top priority for leaders (PwC 2017). We know the employee-organization-customer connections are important, and we know in many cases that leaders are failing at creating the environment for this to happen, so let's look at a few ways Leinwand and Rotering (2016) suggest closing the gap:

1. **Build the strategy.** Similar to the Agile approach of focusing on customer-centered planning and management: Bring customers into the process, honestly assess capabilities, and prepare for disruption.
2. **Translate strategy into the everyday.** Clearly communicate strategy and drive it into every corner of the organization, create visible programs that reinforce the organization's core values, and then connect strategy to budgets and enthusiastically support project and program teams.
3. **Execute strategy.** Connect the work with the strategy every day. Break down silos by creating teams and encouraging ideation and creativity. Keep track of the performance of the leaders and staff,

including successful cross-functional teams and those scaling up strategic activities.

In the case of Apple, while the media might have convinced you that they were an overnight, market-domination juggernaut, in fact, it took decades of experimenting and refining of their processes and culture in preparation for the moment when interest in their products and consumer demand soared. They also experimented with organizational structures by moving from a traditional hierarchy to seamless strategic management and embedded that seamlessness into everything they do. A flat, organizational structure—inhabited by teams innovating, imagining, and prototyping new products and the placing of small bets and market testing their ideas—continues to be core aspects of the Apple culture. By building their organization in this way, these processes and capabilities, along with the work habits that were formed, have consistently paid above-market dividends for years. How will your company build best practices that fit your situation, culture, and capabilities? By taking the time to figure this out and by examining how firms like Apple are building their organizations and developing productive ways to work, you may just wind up with new and improved habits that allow your firm to outperform its competitors for years.

When organizations build a culture that highly values the identification of opportunities, development of core capabilities, and the building of a strong and stable operating core, they are better prepared to scale up as markets open. Developing a broad array of distinctive capabilities can be expensive, involving significant fixed costs and enormous managerial attention. The preferred way to move forward is to focus on a few distinct capabilities and then relentlessly manage them, sharing information, values, and responsibilities across the enterprise (Leinwand and Mainardi 2016).

Lessons Learned:

1. There is value in capacity and capability building. Take the time to create efficient and creative processes capable of scanning for

and evaluating opportunities and executing project plans based on small bets that can blossom into huge wins.

2. Create good management habits. While the conditions of, and motivation for, the development of these capabilities vary from organization to organization, building them and then pushing them out to all corners of your enterprise is an approach to strategy implementation that is likely to lead to distinctiveness and success, a habit worth forming!

Bridging the Gap from Planning and Execution to Strategic Management

While we have identified the importance of bridging the planning to execution gap, a missing piece remains: Once the planners have made the handoff, how do we manage? This is where Agile principles meet strategic management.

The principles of Agile Project Management have been extended into planning and strategic management and serve as the underlying thesis of this book. The term "Agile management" describes the use of Agile principles, originally developed in the software industry, applied to the day-to-day management of all types of enterprises. In the world of project management, Agile principles are most valuable when applied to the management of the triple constraints of projects: Scope, Budget, and Schedule. By working with the customer to develop the *scope* and then applying *budgets* (cost estimates) and timeline impact (*schedule*) to each variation and iteration, the likelihood of overdesign, going over budget, and taking too long is greatly reduced. This process can be used to not only manage projects but is equally as effective when managing enterprises. In my experience, managing in this way results in fewer cost and scheduling issues and a much higher level of customer satisfaction. Let's dig into this question of how Agile project management relates to Agile strategic management in more detail.

When the twelve principles of the Agile Manifesto were created in 2001, the original development team unknowingly described values and principles that were appropriate not just in the managing of projects but in strategic management as well. Here are three of the twelve principles that can be applied directly to Agile management:

1. Organizations are, by their nature, "chaordic," that is, having characteristics of both order and chaos.
2. Trust is the basis for all internal and external relationships.
3. The focus should lie on people first and processes second.

In addition to the above principles, there are also related methods or processes that apply:

1. Iteration—breaking down complexity into manageable chunks.
2. Testing and experimentation—making "small bets" on new strategic initiatives rather than attempting to "change the world" or "boil the ocean."
3. Colocation—carefully building teams and then providing resources.
4. Self-organization—teams with strong players don't need to be managed; let the leaders emerge.
5. Backlogs—allow the "chunks" to form a queue or collection of initiatives that are prioritized and tackled when time and resources allow and/or urgency drives the need.

When I was working on my dissertation, I thought about how chaos and complexity relate to strategy and management, and because of my project management background, I realized the value of using Agile principles to manage the chaos of complicated construction projects could also be effective in general management. It seemed that Agile was a well-suited framework to manage what was an increasingly complicated and more globalized corporate environment. I wondered if my idea was unique and original, or had this connection been made by anyone else? In fact, at this time, it hadn't.

More recently, while searching the Project Management Institute's website (PMI) for literature describing the application of Agile principles to organizational management, after the "No results found" message continually appeared, I did find a few recent articles and a couple of new books that began to bring Agile and management together.

In Steve Denning's *The Age of Agile* (2020) and in Bain & Company consultants Darrell Rigby, Sarah Elk, and Steve Berez's book *Doing Agile Right* (2020), a discussion has begun that attempts to apply Agile principles to management, which are supported by case studies, that suggests that by applying Agile principles to management, organizations outperform those who do not follow this approach. In Denning's case, he views Agile through a leadership lens, and Rigby, Elk, and Berez view it through a balanced approach lens that combines Agile and traditional in discreet areas within an organization. While much of what they say is true, my approach is to converge Agile Planning and Management into one continuous process, and while I have no doubt that Agile thinking can be applied in every functional area, including R&D, operations, leadership, and administrative areas, I have also found that organizations that do so will outperform those that do not. So, how do we do this?

These are the underlying principles of Agile enterprises described by Denning (2020b):

1. Agile enterprises are focused 100% on the customers, with profits the result and not the primary goal of the organization.
2. The organizational structure is mostly self-organizing and team-focused and not hierarchal, with talent and knowledge the most valued competencies.
3. Agile enterprises are responsive, horizontal, innovative, and problem-solving. Leadership and innovation are expected from everyone.

Keep in mind that in Agile software development, iteration and feedback are parts of a continuous work cycle that includes designing, early release, collecting user feedback, redesigning, and improving. As a result, done is never really done. In Agile management, you can use a similar approach in this way: Form teams, evaluate your customers' problems, design products and services to address the problems, develop options, then choose one or more of the options and deliver, measure, and evaluate the outcomes.

According to David Hussman, an Agile coach, after enough iterations, either you are done or you Pivot and move in another direction. Agile management is about following the process described above, preparing for the moment when an opportunity is discovered or a crisis hits, and then being ready to Pivot quickly and seamlessly (Knight 2020). Below is a table that compares the functional characteristics of traditional and Agile software development with Agile management. As you will see, Agile software development and Agile management are similar.

Traditional vs. Agile Development Model plus Agile Management

	Traditional	Agile	Agile Management
Assumptions	Systems are predictable and can be built through extensive planning	Adaptive software can be developed by small teams using continuous design based on rapid feedback	Organizations are comprised of teams in each functional area where collaboration and outcomes are valued
Control	Process-centric	People centric	People, inc. customers, at the center
Management Style	Command-and-control	Leadership & collaboration	Leadership, autonomy & accountability
Roles	Individual, favors specialization	Self-organizing teams encouraging role interchangeability	Leaders lead, team leaders lead teams, staff are empowered, customers participate
Communication	Formal	Informal	Constant, feedback dependent, encouraged
Customer	Important	Critical	Critical, integrated, encouraged
Project Cycle	Task driven, finite	Outcome driven, functionally oriented	Driven by customer needs, integrated, business outcomes focus
Org. Structure	Mechanistic, bureaucratic	Organic, flexible, participative	Matrix design, connectivity is key, outcomes are top priority

As I thought more about how the Agile management process works, it became apparent that the concept of "Pivoting," or making quick and responsive changes based on observations, was the most important step in this approach. Before we get into more details related to Pivoting in the next chapter, let's consider how organizations change direction. Often the result of dropping an unprofitable or unproductive line of business or moving toward something new (e.g., a change in technology, new opportunity, or competitive pressure(s)), this change in direction is accomplished by following an Agile Execution Framework.

Agile Execution Framework

In a 2018 survey by *Forbes* of C-Suite executives, 69% of survey respondents are very or extremely satisfied with strategy, only 55% are satisfied with its execution—a sign that it's easier to design an Agile strategy than implement it. Obstacles to agility, cited by respondents, include competing priorities (67%), a lack of Agile champions (57%) and not knowing how to become Agile (56%).

Before organizations can decide if and when to deploy Agile frameworks to manage their work, leaders need to draw an operating blueprint or plan that configures the staff into cross-functional teams detailing how the teams relate to and support one another, and how they share information across and up and down the enterprise. As described elsewhere, teams are best served to start on a pilot project that requires the sharing of expertise that already exists within the organization and includes the customer in its plans. Agile organizations take the form of what Mintzberg described as "innovative adhocracies," where an assemblage of creative, functional teams of experts are focused on highly dynamic settings, environments, and situations. These teams are loosely coupled with each having its own mission, complementing the missions of other teams, and all working toward an end product contributing to the overall value generated on behalf of the organization. This team-based approach is organized into two groups: 1)

Core, or shared expertise, and 2) Enabling, value-added and idea-generating, both of which complement one another and drive the organization's strategy. According to McKinsey & Company, the organization needs to make four decisions to effectively coordinate the work of the two groups (Core and Enabling) to create maximum value:

1. Decide where profit and loss lie.
2. Decide how incentives are designed when teams don't own P&L.
3. Agree on a coordinating framework for the work of the team.
4. Consider how culture needs to be adapted to make this structure work.

They suggest that the Core teams set priorities and are P&L responsible, and the Enabling teams drive the activities against the priorities set by the Core teams (Comella-Dorda, Handscomb, and Zaidi 2020). In order to make this structure work, requirements need to be clearly defined and well-connected to both the Core and Enabling teams: 1) a well-run planning and strategy communication process needs to be put in place and 2) the organization's willingness to empower, make accountable, and create a customer service mindset—all keys to these Agile and innovative structures working efficiently and creating maximum value.

While management approaches and frameworks emphasize the translation of objectives and strategies into activities and output, mostly identified through the strategic planning process, when Agile principles are blended with the outputs of an institutionalized asymmetric learning process, the best of both worlds come together. Using Agile Strategy Manager, a well-established strategy tool and information platform, organizations are able to "reconfigure strategy, structure, processes, people, and technology quickly toward value creation and value protection" (Singhal 2020). Through a process best described as virtual and continuous, teams follow a pathway consisting of observation, planning, testing, feedback, and executive review. And since Agile teams have accountability as a core principle, tracking and measuring outcomes is as important a part of the process as is flexibility and ideation. In this way of working, ideas are encouraged and tested, the feedback of the customer is included in both the planning and testing phases, and the organization has the information it needs to decide which new programs to invest in and which to let go.

Quite a few of the tasks included within the Agile Strategy Manager process align with and supplement a number of the more well-known strategy frameworks (e.g., SWOT, PEST, and SMART) and are useful in the capture of information and insights, the generation of new ideas resulting from a robust planning process, and, finally, the tracking of progress and performance. In many cases, the launch of such a program is less of a software and systems challenge and more of a cultural change—but well worth the effort.

Here are a few suggestions to remake strategy so it becomes a powerful tool in your arsenal when facing disruption and intense competition:

- First, drop older, more linear approaches to strategy, including the annual planning retreat and budgeting meetings. Strategy is an ongoing process and not an annual event.
- Second, build a continuous cycle of evaluation, adjustment, approval, and monitoring of results. Discuss performance reports regularly. Build accountability.
- Third, closely observe the external, competitive environment and bring that intelligence into the review cycle. In my strategy meetings, I have each attendee share an insight or some trend information that is relevant to the business.
- Fourth, communicate any revisions to the strategic plan in an abbreviated form (e.g., one to two pages) to all stakeholders so everyone is on board and in sync.

The trick to building a strategic organization is to directly invest in the strategy formulation and implementation processes and support this work on a continuous basis with data, observations, and analysis. When combined with your team's insights, this process can help inform when adjustments and strategy overhauls are needed and keep you on track (Collaborative Strategy 2020b).

Chapter 13

THE KEY TO SUCCESS: PLANNING TO PIVOT

"Pivot. 1. To change directions but stay grounded in what
we have learned. 2. A structured course correction designed
to test a new fundamental hypothesis about a product,
strategy, and engine of growth."
—Innolution

A s the definition suggests, a "Pivot" is a change in direction or strategy, or a "course correction" without a change in vision (Reis 2012). While I agree with that generally, I would also add that the change in direction or strategy or a course correction should be "the result of systematic environmental scanning or industry conditions." There needs to be thoughtful consideration for those conditions that need to be present in order for teams to consider a Pivot. In the context of pharmaceutical drug development, Mike Rea said that while in the R&D process, companies need to remain flexible or "loose" and ready to Pivot in pursuit of another path or opportunity, suggesting that the ability to make better decisions while progressing is a winning strategy (Rea 2020). This combination of research and analysis, decision-making, and execution is at the core of Agile management.

> *"Agile is the ability of an organization to renew itself,*
> *adapt, change quickly, and succeed in a rapidly*
> *changing, ambiguous, turbulent environment."*
> —Aaron De Smet, McKinsey & Company

In the context of organizational strategy, a Pivot is meant to signal the redirection of activities, focus, and resources away from an activity or project(s), often underperforming and/or not meeting performance targets, and toward a more important and urgent activity. It identifies a critical inflection point when events and conditions are such that the organization needs to make a quick and informed shift from one direction, or strategic initiative or direction or set of activities, to another. For Pivoting to work, organizations need to prepare for a Pivot, outline the circumstances by which they should Pivot, what steps need to be taken to Pivot, and finally, decide how Pivots will be assessed for effectiveness.

> *"Clarity, ruthless prioritization, and preparing to change*
> *direction, are the cornerstones of agile decision-making"*
> —Simon Hayward

In the world of start-ups, a Pivot is used to describe companies that were founded on a certain vision and then, as a result of some experience or market reaction or consumer review, usually a bad one, Pivot to another business. In the customer development process described by consultant Eric Reiss, he details how the entrepreneur is constantly tinkering with the business model in the hopes of tightly matching the model with the customers' needs. This process includes a feedback loop that, in addition to providing real-time performance data, informs the company as to whether to stay the course or Pivot. He suggests that if a start-up doesn't find a profitable and scalable model, it will likely go out of business, making the search for a better model urgent and the preparation for Pivoting intense. Since the frenetic pace of start-ups can be described as Chaos + Speed + Pivots = Success, the search for a workable model continues with founders often making multiple Pivots, some small adjustments, and some major changes (Blank 2010).

Lessons Learned:
1. Start-ups continually search for a repeatable and scalable business model.
2. Most start-up business models are initially wrong.
3. The process of iteration and Pivoting are keys in search of the successful model.
4. Pivots need to happen quickly, rapidly, and often.
5. Pivots are why start-ups need to be Agile and opportunistic.

There are quite a few examples of companies founded on one idea and then, after piloting and collecting customer data, Pivoting to a different model and, in some cases, a very different business. Here are some examples.

- YouTube started as a dating site designed to allow users to upload video and then, because users found the video uploading functionality useful, Pivoted away from the dating focus toward video sharing and what is now the dominant video sharing site in the world.
- Flickr started as an online video gaming site and then Pivoted to a photo uploading site.
- Odeo was initially a podcasting company and then reinvented itself and launched Twitter.
- PayPal started as a digital to cellphone sharing site and Pivoted to online payments.

In all these examples, the companies had an original vision, and through a process of trial and error and collecting and analyzing user feedback, exchanged the original vision for something new, and in doing so, Pivoted into very different, world-class mega-companies.

How Do Organizations Pivot?

At this point, the benefits of being prepared to Pivot, knowing what conditions are present leading up to a Pivot, how to execute Pivots, and why Pivoting is an important capability for organizations operating in volatile and dynamic environments seem obvious. Why? Because markets change. What was once clear when the plan was formed is now changing and increasingly unclear—and organizations struggle to adapt. If you wait until trouble appears to begin to think about Pivoting, it is almost always too late. In some situations, customers' needs change, and as a result, leaders and teams need to rapidly look for better, faster ways of meeting emerging customer needs and expectations. Giving teams the resources and support needed to come up with innovative solutions is the leader's job, with the ability to innovate vital to success (Horrigan 2020).

What Does a Pivot Look Like? A Few Examples.

Calling an Audible

> *"Call an audible: To decide what to do at the last second after seeing all possible options and obstacles that come up. Comes from football, seen when the quarterback goes up to the line of scrimmage, sees a defensive alignment he wasn't expecting, and adjusts by yelling out a new play."*
> —Urban Dictionary

In some cases, Pivoting can be like audibles in football where the quarterback changes the play that was called in the huddle while standing at the line of scrimmage based on his scan of the field and on-the-spot analysis of the likelihood of its success or failure. Based on his instantaneous assessment, the play is changed as necessary. That split-second decision is usually made by only the most experienced quarterbacks who have the coach's confidence. This instantaneous decision-making process is experienced by executives every day. What can we learn from athletes?

The Game Slows Down, Being in the Zone, Developing Flow

In a 2013 interview, Tony Romo, the former quarterback for the Dallas Cowboys, said that "the game still slows down more for me every year I am in the league," describing being in the zone, time slowing down, and getting into the flow.

Physiologically, this phenomenon has scholarly roots. For some, the game appears slower as the amount of information is processed by the brain at a faster rate. Researchers at University College London suggested that the sensation of time slowing, or reaction time becoming enhanced, is felt even more so among elite athletes. Often referred to as "flow," this is an optimal state that occurs when there is a balance between perceived challenges of a situation and a person's skills or capabilities to manage action. These flow experiences are often accompanied by an order of consciousness where the ability to concentrate increases, and the person feels in control of the performance.

Psychologist Erika Carlson suggests that this skill has to do with pattern recognition. The brain has literally mapped the situations, so these athletes are able to recognize what's coming at them. Does the game slow down for leaders who are responsible for scanning markets, industries, and competition and then developing and implementing strategy? Do they develop an ability to recognize patterns? I say yes to all, and here's why and how.

A Sixth Sense

"Lateral vision is as important in #management as it is in sport. We can no more play basketball with our eyes fixated on the net than can we manage an organization with our eyes fixated on a screen."
—Henry Mintzberg, @Mintzberg141

While this book is not about leadership per se, to some extent, strategy is leadership, and leadership is strategy. Strategic implementation is largely based on the intuitive nature of an organization's leader and the leader's ability to recognize and exploit subtle changes in the marketplace using what we are calling Pivots. Similar to the experiences shared by "playmakers" in basketball, quarterbacks in football, and chess masters, when these elite athletes see the field and sense where the action might lead, they are able to "skate to where the puck is going rather than skating to where the puck is." Leaders demonstrate some of these same abilities.

While leaders may not be trained to have intuition or be intuitive, that ability can be developed over time. In the book *A Sense of Where You Are*, author John McPhee recalls a conversation with Bill Bradley, the former Princeton University and New York Knicks basketball player and US Senator (McPhee 1978). When Bradley was asked about an amazing play where he tossed the ball over his shoulder without looking at the basket and the ball went in, Bradley said, "When you have played basketball for a while, you don't need to look at the basket when you are in close like this. You develop a sense of where you are." Of course, this intuition or sense is the result of thousands of hours of shooting drills, practices, and games. I believe it is the same for leaders.

Effective and successful leaders often mention having a "sense" of leading, the result of years of reading and studying, coupled with experience and situational familiarity. As mentioned above, Erika Carlson would say that leaders develop an ability to recognize patterns. Today, when information is coming at a rapid-fire rate and change is continuous and disruptive, leaders need to have the basic training and developed skills and all of those tools necessary to be successful, plus a strong dose of what Bill Bradley refers to as a "sense of where you are."

Pivoting and Asymmetric Learning

When do organizations Pivot? While some Pivoting occurs when situations change or conditions emerge that force rapid change, other Pivots can be linked to preprogrammed conditions or outcomes. How do organizations prepare? By developing scenarios as part of the planning process, they are able to recognize future market, industry, political, and economic conditions and then link these predictors to potential future Pivots. In order to do this, planners need to 1) talk to customers, vendors, and suppliers to understand their perspectives on the future, 2) invest the time and energy in a PEST analysis as a way to visualize economic, political, regulatory, supply chain, and technological disruption ahead, 3) keep a close eye out for competitors and potential up-starts (smalls heading in your direction), 4) understand industry trends, and 5) be on the lookout for potentially disruptive events that could affect your business. Anything can happen, so imagining what's ahead, documenting events that could impact your business, and then coming up with plans to respond to the changed conditions will keep everyone in the organization engaged and aware of what to do should the industry, environment, political, or technology conditions rapidly change. Discussing these conditions, sharing a vision of the future, and playing out scenarios and what-ifs is, in and of itself, a strategic and valuable process!

As mentioned, Pivots can be planned for and often follow scenario analyses where "if-then" models are manipulated to predict various outcomes (e.g., if the economy expands by x%, and we are profitable at the rate of y%, we will invest in these new projects). But not all Pivots are created equal. Some are responses to changed conditions, and others are not. In some cases, you can discover that your firm is selling the wrong product to the wrong customer, and if you want to stay in business, it's time to Pivot! Sometimes there's a change in the marketplace that requires an adjustment, feature change, or function improvement. Some are market-driven, and some are customer-driven. Some are small and some large. Maybe a tweak will do if the firm can modify an existing product or service, but if the customer needs you to develop a new, high-value service rather than a cookie-cutter, low-cost version, a Pivot may be needed to refocus on customized products or services. These examples are all Pivots. As you might remember from the 1990s, when streaming services eliminated vinyl and taped music, the disruption that took place required record companies to reinvent themselves or go out of business. This was a serious Pivot.

The ability to Pivot quickly and proactively is a critical capability that organizations need to develop to ensure continuity and ongoing business operations. The capacity to Pivot requires three capabilities: 1) the ability to identify the need to Pivot, 2) the ability to assess the right level of Pivot response, and 3) executing the Pivot appropriately. If you agree, your company should invest in developing the processes, tools, technologies, and the employee skills and capabilities required to ensure survival before you are faced with an existential threat or new crisis (Collaborative Strategy 2020a).

Asymmetric Management

"Molecules, like people, are unpredictable."
—Mike Rea

When organizations accept that prediction can be both a false assurance and a commitment to a process of uncovering opportunities, being aware of the risks while planning creates both healthy skepticism and openness to new ideas. By creating options in a process Rea describes as asymmetric learning, teams are likely to produce "differentiated insights" that may be valuable, unique, and lead to competitive advantage. When your firm develops this process as a work habit and as a core value, the harnessing of the cumulative brainpower of an organization by creating and encouraging asymmetric teams is to develop a continuous stream of new ideas faster and more creatively than the competition (Rea 2020). This is at the heart of ideation and creative planning.

By developing this learning capability and the associated work habits, managers are able to resist locking in on singular, predicted solutions and remain open to opportunities, insights, and new ideas. This is where the gold lies. If teams are open to new ideas and continuously loop them back into the system, then risks and opportunities are evaluated and managed, and the organization learns. Leaders need to guide but not stifle. They should ask the team what resources are needed to support their work and then provide what Rea refers to as "permeable guide rails" that function as the outer limits of the organization's commitment and investment (e.g., timeline, current goal/target, and available resources) (Rea 2020). Ask questions but resist predicting outcomes. Create "serendipitous opportunities" by design and not by accident. When teams generate great ideas, organizations find the need to move away from one activity toward another—to Pivot. The art of the Pivot is based on the willingness of the actors in an organization to accept that some things are possible, and more are revealed when teams are provided with the resources and soft boundaries to do their best work without tightly written, preprogrammed outcomes. "Pivoting" is a state of mind, an approach, and an awareness of the possible. It is more art than science. More feel than process. It requires commitment and practice.

Since asymmetry is, by its very nature, iterative and creative, providing lots of options and insights—with some coming as part of the planning process and others coming from the field as production teams get a sense of the market's reaction to new product and services—how will organizations manage the process of choosing a new idea or shifting away from an existing one? They would certainly benefit from following these next two steps to move from idea to initiative: 1) Create a process for evaluating and approving new ideas and projects, and then 2) use a system or software program that helps organize and manage the big categories of responsibility (e.g., goals, timeline, resources needed, and performance expectations), along with the collection of smaller bits of information that all become part of evaluating how much to invest, or continue to invest or disinvest, in any project. Once the plan is approved and ready to be put into the field, the handoff is made between the planners and doers, following the principles of Agile management.

Who and Where Are the Practitioners?

There are groups of practitioners, scholars, and others trying to improve planning approaches to make them more responsive, data-driven, and objective, all trying to find the best solution to planning problems that help with prediction and decision-making. One such gathering, the bi-annual International Conference on Automated Planning and Scheduling, hosts competitions of researchers and planners to build new and improved planning systems with one core principle that is widely agreed upon: Even the best planning algorithms still aren't as effective as human beings with an aptitude for problem-solving (Hardesty 2017). The challenge for these scientists is to convert the insights of those practitioners who are truly excellent at planning to a machine-based process capable of sharing their insights and approach to planning more broadly. Currently, the work in automated planning is attempting to interpret a user's high-level strategy into a form that makes it more useful for the machine to process and analyze. Using natural language processing to make the system fully automatic, the work to convert human descriptions of these high-level strategies into linear temporal logic continues. The world of automated planning, including scenarios, forecasting, and prediction—largely dependent on AI—is clearly ahead with the role of managing the system left to the human experts.

Mintzberg emphasized the value of human involvement in planning. He wrote that formal systems grounded in data analytics could certainly process more information faster and that while "they can consolidate it, aggregate it, and move it about....they can never internalize it, comprehend it, synthesize it" (Mintzberg 1994). The need for humans in the design of systems and the analysis and interpretation of the data remains a key component of any planning work. The use of AI in planning needs to be approached cautiously and as a supportive activity and not the primary source of decision-making for planners. As Ray Dalio, the founder of Bridgewater Associates, the world's largest hedge fund, suggests, AI-driven analytics can help us "get above our emotional attachments to our own conclusions," but it can also cause dependency on the machine for outcomes (Hill 2019). It seems most useful to treat AI or data-driven conclusions as second opinions that can be used to spot trends and calculate scenarios. Still, it remains the domain of humans to apply judgment and intuition to the calculations in order to make the final decision.

PART 5:

Imagine, Create, and Plan to Succeed

Chapter 14

TOOLS FOR MANAGING COMPLEX ORGANIZATIONS

O rganizations need to plan, to observe changes in their industries and the world, imagine possible and probable futures, track their activities and goals, and adjust their plans as conditions change. Many leaders find this process exhausting, difficult, and incoherent, often relying on their own intuition and gravitas to make strategic decisions. This is truly the hard work of leading. For those leaders and managers ready to get on with it, there are tools in the business intelligence and technology markets that are capable of organizing, reporting, and providing virtual information that can help understand performance today and plan for the future. These tools provide the structure, tracking, and rapid calculation that allows for fast and effective decision-making, Agile responses, and multidirectional communication. What leaders need to do is make the commitment of human and technological resources to planning and implementation. Here are some tools that are vitally important for planning.

Strategy Execution Management (SEM), an approach to strategy execution that starts with a set of processes and leads to strategy execution as an embedded system, is a combination of both, resulting in capabilities that include:

195

- Strategy visualization
- Mapping of strategy and metrics to future plans and projects underway
- Tracking of benefits planned against benefits generated
- Alignment of individual roles to the achievement of specific strategies

These efforts require a strong commitment to the process as technologies continue to evolve and support other IT systems, Agile management activities, digital portfolio management, and the mapping of investments to performance, outcomes, and value-add. Developing a continuous and fluid connection between the planners and the implementers, as business strategy evolves and the velocity of business increases, is enabled by SEM technologies. Thankfully, once the scenarios are thoroughly described, reviewed, and documented, and the performance measurements related to each of the Endstates have been defined, there are a fairly large number of software tools in the market to help manage an organization's strategies, priorities, and performance.

In Gartner's 2019 Market Guide for Strategy Execution, more than twenty representative companies specializing in Strategic Execution Management (SEM) software platforms were listed (Stang and Handler 2020). Clearly, organizations are reaching out for technology and expertise to wrestle with this challenge.

Strategic Execution Management

SEM technologies can help communicate an organization's strategy and determine the degree to which people are doing something in support of strategic objectives. SEM tools indicate the degree to which people, ongoing projects, and ongoing assets are delivering the desired results or how the strategy is being executed and goals achieved. The timing of strategy execution makes a difference. Although SEM is important to long-term survival, aiming execution-related actions toward the next quarter's performance goals becomes paramount in some cases. In cases where short-term demands, often in the form of operational goals such as quarterly results, interfere with strategic goals, the strategic goals will always be less important. In the Gartner Report, the authors suggest IT be bifurcated into strategic and operational units to avoid conflict between strategic and operational priorities. While I certainly agree, this same structure would be beneficial at the organizational level as well. Keeping the strategic and operational units separate helps ensure that strategic priorities are, in fact, completed (Gartner 2019).

Now more than ever, systems and processes need to be tight, lean, and responsive. There is no time (or bytes) to waste. Few capabilities focus Agile like a strong analytics program that helps determine where a team should focus, from one Agile iteration (sprint) to the next. Successful analytics are rarely hard to understand and are often startling in their clarity, which suggests, according to Professor Alex Cowan from the Darden School of Business, that "having the right technology is not only a competitive advantage but essential for survival" (Cowan 2020).

In the short term, SEM tools will be developed that include more simplistic and dynamic dashboards, portfolio management features, and effective measurements that collect and display business-level outcomes. As Gartner (2019) suggests, these "must-have" features should include bidirectional communications, program management, and formal scenario planning functionality. Over the next three to five years, best-in-class SEM programs will include capabilities such as capacity planning, strategic decision support, business process tracking, and asset tracking. The bottom line: Organizations need to evaluate their strategic execution capabilities sooner than later. Are the programs and systems working together? Can you get the information you need when you need it? Are the systems helping your people work faster and smarter? Organizations would be well-served to take the time to improve information flow, streamline, and simplify. While automation is certainly growing in relevance and utility for managers, it is also an evolving capability for planners. Fortunately, there are tools available to help organize the work and track progress. Let's consider a few.

Strategic Execution Management Software

Agile management, the single and continuous process that applies Agile principles to planning and management, is driven by lots of information and data that require collection, categorization, modeling, and evaluation. In current strategy literature, "Strategy Execution," closely related to Agile management, has the best collection of tools and techniques that can be adapted to Agile management. Sophisticated strategy execution management requires tools that connect the goals and objectives as detailed in the planning process, with those assigned to product teams charged with executing the activities, responsible for measuring performance, and driving business value.

As with any strategic decision, communication and consensus-building are both critical to successful implementation, but tools are critical for the aggregation of data and the production of unbiased analyses. Referred to as SEM tools, buyers seek to connect their strategies, metrics, and resources with the actual, anticipated results of plans, programs, and assets.

Other tools that are helpful to product management teams include team collaboration programs, communication tools, project management software, and "low-code platforms" designed to create, and in some cases connect, enterprise applications fast. In Agile, speed is essential to business success, and as often is the case, the company able to move fastest to solve a problem wins (*Business Matters* 2020). Businesses need to develop the capability to develop solutions and deliver applications fast enough to keep pace with business demands and the competition. The low code approach allows rapid solution development by utilizing existing, tested APIs and scripts that can be cut and pasted into new applications. In this continuous Agile process, stakeholders can push change forward by driving frequent modifications to solutions that constantly produce value.

Artificial Intelligence

Another area of planning and automation is a branch of artificial intelligence focused on the realization of strategies and actions, known as "Automation and Planning," or just "AI Planning." AI Planning focuses on the realization of strategies typically limited to intelligent agents, robots, and unmanned vehicles, but with many of the technologies and applications directly relatable to planning. The underlying principle at work is that in dynamically unknown environments, strategy needs to be revised on the fly and evaluated prior to execution, with models and policies developed and adapted for immediate use. AI Planning is an exciting area of research and a potential point of convergence for planning and management where plans can be put in the field, and after data is collected, changes can be made on the fly. As you can see, speed, accuracy, learning, and adaptation are being aggregated into increasingly smart platforms and tools.

While the goal of planning is to identify goals and then a set of action steps, AI Planning can be described as the simplification of a complex multiple variable process. In its simplest form, the "Classical Planning Problem" is the initial state of clarity where an organization's situation, after taking the action steps, can be accurately predicted. In more complex planning approaches, with undetermined actions or other events outside the control of the agent or planner, the output begins to move from the linear and simple to the more complex, similar to a tree, and each branch representing strategic initiatives and related action steps. In the planning domain, the best way to manage these multivariate models is by using software programs that model scenarios and potential outcomes. Once the models have been used repeatedly and adjusted over time, they become increasingly accurate, which, in theory, could produce "smart algorithms" able to process variation and provide directionally valid possibilities.

Algorithms

In the realm of planning algorithms, there are many discreet algorithmically powered models being used (e.g., Classical, Temporal, Probabilistic,

Preference-based, Conditional, Contingent, and Conformant with the most well-known, SPSS or Spike, being used by the Hubble Space Telescope). Each of these algorithms is designed to solve planning problems in different environments and conditions. As you can see, when technologies are brought to planning, it gets very complex, very quickly. As a result, well-trained smart teams need to be involved from the start in modeling, visioning, scenario development, and option analyses, and why AI is needed to manage the data and determine possibilities.

> *"Artificial Intelligence creates real strategic dilemmas."*
> —Andrew Hill

Will the future of planning involve the development of software tools that take the form of an algorithm(s) and powered by AI that could model the future, track changing conditions, and alert management teams when the potential exists for some kind of negative consequences? Recently, just such an algorithm was developed by Harvard's Machine Intelligence Lab at Boston's Children's Hospital designed for use in "the prediction of outbreaks about two weeks before they occur, in time to put effective containment measures in place." Described as a disease-tracking model or tool, different scenarios are projected based on assumptions made upfront, and then responses are suggested to make immediate changes in behaviors. It functions as a thermostat in a cooling or heating system to guide intermittent activation or relaxation of public health interventions" (Carey 2020). In another example from the same industry, the pandemic has activated many new modeling programs that are designed to sense changing viral spread patterns and alert researchers of the likelihood of out-of-control dispersion.

Scenarios

It's not a great leap to imagine this line of thinking could be of help to organizations. Of course, taking on a platform development project of this type and magnitude will require an executive-level commitment of time and staff resources in order to design an array of scenarios or "what-ifs," along with a system capable of updating that feeds data into the machine, making it "smarter" and the output increasingly useful. An early warning system would be invaluable when changed conditions warrant attention. The future is here, and organizations are already working on just such a system.

Scenarios and Planning

One potential technique to help planners and organizations visualize the future is "strategic backcasting," a process used to reverse-engineer preferred future states. It begins with imagining an ideal future state and then works backward to identify policies and actions necessary to connect that vision of the future with the present.

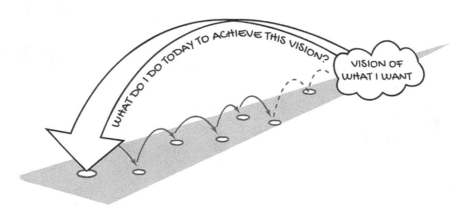

1. BEGIN WITH THE ENDSTATE IN MIND

2. WORK BACKWARDS FROM THE VISION TO PRESENT

3. DETERMINE STEPS NECESSARY TO ACHIEVE THE VISION

4. GET TO WORK!

While forecasting involves the prediction of the future based on current trends, backcasting approaches the challenge of considering the future from the opposite direction. The future desired state is envisioned, and steps are defined to get to that future state rather than following the current, often incremental, path toward undefined goals.

Another potential for future planning is to convene scenario planning activities or workshops and use data from your organization and industry, and other related industries, to build narratives that describe plausible futures. By building and mapping scenarios, planning teams can better understand next-order impacts, develop new products and services, and create strategic visions for their organizations. Sometimes part of a design-thinking exercise, scenarios can be used to test theories for strategic change based on internally and externally driven conditions. Here is an example of what the artifact might look like borrowed from Anthros Consulting (2020).

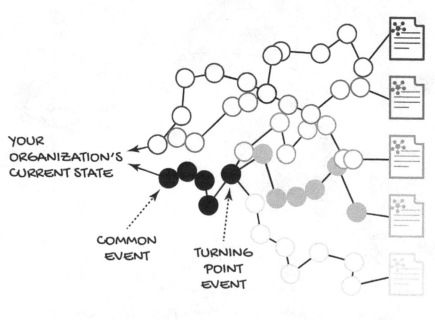

In the above and below examples, "by using a scenario-based method to enable organizations" to imagine a future of options and possibilities, "organizations can explore divergent futures and produce Agile, adaptable strategic plans and implementation." By planning and mapping various paths forward, when the time comes for a Pivot, the organization's leaders will be able to "change course sooner and without a time-consuming decision-making process" (Anthros Consulting 2020).

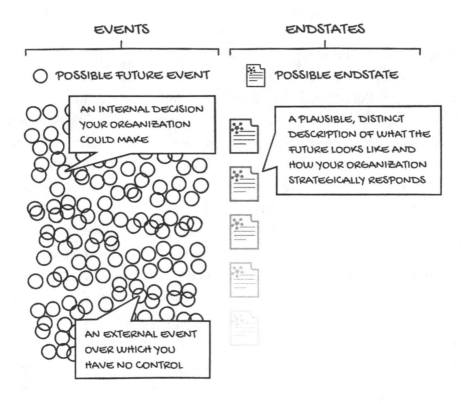

The value of these scenario-planning exercises is to bring multiple insights and automation to the planning process and drive teams to think about what is possible and necessary to deliver desired results. By using custom-designed algorithms, companies like Anthros Consulting are able to use data visualization techniques, along with Business Intelligence, MS Excel, Tableau, machine learning, and other sophisticated data management tools to collect, model, and share insights across multiple platforms, operating units, and leadership teams.

Simulation

Monte Carlo simulations utilize powerful computer programs to repeat random samplings in order to generate a range of possible outcomes. Used to describe probability, the output reports both the range of values a variable might take and the likelihood of those values occurring. The most commonly used probability distribution used for modeling business uncertainty is the triangular distribution that is defined by three points: minimum, likely, and maximum values. For example, you may be programming a simple point of sale app that has taken from ten days best case, twelve days likely, and fifteen days worst case to complete, based on past experience. Since probability can be calculated for each of the three points, the simulation is able to plot a range of probabilities in a normal distribution or bell-shaped curve, so you are able to get a realistic picture of the likelihood of the app being delivered on time and on budget.

As an add-on to scenario analysis, Monte Carlo simulations can run an infinite number of probabilities and sensitivities on variables entered by the planning team and, while the project is underway, the management team. Certainly, no one should assume these simulations can predict the future, but they are useful as peeks through the keyhole to a world of possibilities. What is possible? Where can we exploit the future? What should we do to align these possibilities and the organization's capabilities?

Clearly, there is a new day dawning in strategic planning. By empowering planning teams to consider an organization's future state and then applying any one or more of the technologies described above, any number of possibilities can be tested and evaluated before moving ahead. This is a glimpse into the future of strategic planning.

Chapter 15

NEW IDEAS AND NEXT STEPS: THE FUTURE OF STRATEGIC MANAGEMENT

"We need to be surfing and not sitting on a beach chair."
—Anonymous

The world is changing, fast. How do we survive uncertainty and complexity? There is growing pessimism in the markets as global GDP slows, the COVID-19 pandemic continues its grip on the world, and uncertainty reigns. In a recent survey of global CEOs, PwC reports that more than half believe GDP will decline and have decreased confidence in their company's twelve-month growth prospects. They have shifted from record optimism to record pessimism in areas such as potential trade conflicts, cyber threats, and policy uncertainty (PwC CEP 2020). What is clear is the growing pervasiveness of the internet, the need for technology-related regulation, the challenges to source talent in the form of skilled new hires and the upskilling of existing workers capable of working in an increasingly technical and complex environment, and the imminent threat of climate change—all exponentially increasing the challenges to planners, leaders, and managers.

In 2013, two young Oxford University researchers published a paper stating that roughly half of US jobs were "at risk of computerization," igniting a debate that has steadily climbed up the CEO agenda. PwC's own analysis of more than 200,000 jobs in twenty-nine countries—although less foreboding—confirms that 30% of jobs are potentially subject to automation by the mid-2030s and that workers with lower education levels will be hardest hit initially" (Frey and Osborne 2013). As a result, organizations of every type, size, and location will need to move faster, smarter, and with more flexibility as situations shift and change around the world. It is in this faster, smarter, and flexible context that Agile management enters the picture as a solid and responsive approach for leaders and managers to consider.

As a result of the COVID-19 pandemic, the world's socioeconomic relationships have become very clear. No one is immune from the challenges facing a world that is interconnected and interdependent as never before. In an era of economic and global disruption, new ways to plan and manage are becoming increasingly valuable with flexibility, capabilities, and the ability to Pivot when conditions change the difference between survival and extinction for many organizations. Companies need to Pivot quickly to fill urgent needs with recent, poignant examples, including the urgent need for ventilators, hand sanitizer, and face masks. While most organizations understand this to some extent, in a recent survey by the Business Agility Institute, 71% of the companies surveyed thought they had low business agility and acknowledged needing to invest more in training executives and staff about the approach (Business Agility Institute 2019).

In the previous chapters, I've tried to describe the challenges of planning and managing organizations in the twenty-first century in this era of intense complexity and change. The pace of work and need for flexibility and responsiveness is nothing short of frenetic, some of which is occurring as a result of globalization, ubiquitous communications, and the increasing speed attributed to the commoditization of software and the maturing and stabilization of computer systems. The question to consider is: How does all of this affect planning?

Looking Back to See What's Ahead

In order to understand the future, we took a brief look back at the history of strategy and planning. We took a short sojourn through the history of strategy in strategic planning from the early twentieth century and the Age of Industrialization and Frederick Taylor, to the 1970s, to the 1990s and the era of strategy scholarship led by scholars such as Henry Mintzberg, Michael Porter, Peter Senge, and others who studied and wrote and taught their way through a changing strategy landscape having to do with increasingly complex, human behavior-driven themes resulting in emergent and adaptive understanding and approaches to strategy. In the early twenty-first century, researchers like Margaret Wheatley, Marc Cutright, James Gleick, and others realized that the serial and structured nature of the late twentieth-century theories were no longer adequate for contemporary organizations, which were now vastly larger and more complex, operating globally in different time zones and across cultures. They began adapting principles of chaos and complexity theory based on laws existing within the natural environment into new ways of planning and managing organizations.

At the beginning of the third decade of the twenty-first century, I find myself wondering if things will ever stop moving so fast. The often-used metaphor for managing, "building the plane while flying the plane," seems apropos as we move into an era of continuous planning and strategy and management. There's no reason to believe that the world will not continue to speed up and complexity compound, so the questions for us, as managers and leaders, are: What do we do? How do we manage? How do we cope?

The writing of this book began when I needed a plan in order to decide the direction of a newly launched company almost forty years ago. Since then, over and over, in various stops along a career that spanned corporate America and higher education, working side-by-side a number of very smart and successful bosses, I noticed that very few relied on planning with fewer seeming to plot a course or direction ahead of time. Rather, most preferred to fly by the seat of their pants, to switch and change direction as inspiration struck and opportunities appeared. It became increasingly obvious to me that some combination of the two, a deliberate plan, along with the ability to shift and change and react to changed conditions, made the most sense for leaders and managers. So, how does planning fit with this perspective?

I've worked for corporate and academic leaders, one a well-known strategy scholar, most of whom were very experienced in running complicated organizations, and frankly, it still surprises me that to this day, many (most?) leaders place very little value on plans and planning. In a recent discussion with a coaching client, and in response to his being overwhelmed by the constant shifting and changing of priorities, I suggested some of this could be attributed to not having a plan that, among other benefits, could provide the context for some of these decisions and reduce the constant "Why don't we try this?" He told me he "knew it was important" but would likely "not have time for that for a while." Being very familiar with the typical small business owner who is juggling as fast as he/she can, I suggested hiring a consultant to lead a brief but much-needed planning exercise, to which he responded, "I'll get to it after all of these other priorities are taken care of."

Whether its laziness, a lack of accountability, or a lack of understanding of the value of the process and the plan, the simple truth is that planning—where staff and employees, leaders, and customers get together on a regular and systematic basis and share observations, multiple perspectives, and experiences—seems to be the right formula for success, regardless of size or industry. The combination of planning that is organized around maximizing current successes, visualizing a future state and testing new ideas, followed by Pivoting as new information is uncovered, creates a rich and open process where ideas and insights and people are valued and appreciated. This process is core to the Agile management process.

Over the years, in my role as a leader and manager, and when confronted with uncertainty, I have talked to thought leaders, sought new ideas and approaches from writers and scholars, read self-help books, hired executive advisors, and taken mindfulness and stress reduction classes.

I've taken every opportunity to learn how to adapt to the relentless wave of decisions that need to be made while managing large, complex organizations and have shared my research and current thinking in the pages of this book. For some, the challenge is overwhelming and comparable to the sentiment expressed by Alvin Toffler, who in the early 1970s produced a book and film titled *Future Shock*, and Judith Butler, contemporary feminist philosopher, both suggesting that "life will be livable but may not be bearable." For leaders, this seems more truth than fiction, and while I don't necessarily agree with the direness of the message, I do agree that leading and managing will become increasingly challenging, fast, and complicated. Whether it's bearable is up to you. What I can offer are some ideas to help you cope.

Pattern Recognition and Intuition

"Leaders need to manage the complex geometry of ideas."
—Mike Rea (2021)

In Michael Lewis's book *Premonition* (2021), he looks back at the pandemic and how the US government functioned—or didn't—in the face of the crisis. It is an enlightening peek into the implications of fast-moving, dynamically unstable situations occurring within a bureaucracy unable, unwilling, or unprepared to accept and manage an impending crisis with global mortality and economic implications. In this story, the readers are provided a roadmap to what Lewis describes as apophenia, or the tendency to perceive meaningful connections between unrelated things, as the key for the protagonist's ability to see the pandemic coming. In earlier parts of this book, discussions related to pattern recognition and managing, pattern recognition and leading, social network analysis, and the ability to see changes in systems and taking actions to influence or correct the trajectory and speed of those changes were described and analyzed. In the case of the pandemic, despite a number of scientists seeing the patterns related to the impending pandemic, government leaders failed to take any actions, and as a result, many lives were lost.

As described in a number of higher ed case studies I've written, sometimes leaders will rely on their intuition to make decisions, often leading to arbitrary and frequently changing strategies. In these cases, a lack of accountability for outcomes, along with incoherent goals and performance measures, were significant contributing factors to the leader's disregard for strategic planning and underwhelming outcomes.

There is, however, more to intuition than leaders making arbitrary decisions. In Daniel Kahneman's book *Thinking, Fast and Slow* (2011), he found a distinction between two different kinds of intuition: System 1, which is automatic and quick (intuition), and System 2, a slower and more deliberate activity. For leaders and managers, it is likely to require a combination of both Systems to be most effective. Why does this matter? If conditions require leaders to be more intuitive, along with the other suggested steps described elsewhere in the book (e.g., developing smart teams, scanning the environment for change, recognizing patterns, etc.), then developing a greater sense of intuition, at least for day-to-day decisions and in between the more formal strategy discussions, is worth considering. To hone your intuition, you need to be deliberate at accumulating information, developing beliefs, and operating in continuous learning mode. The combination of intuition and deep thought is called for, and there is a place for both in the leadership-management-Agile worlds.

Agile Organizations Are Best Equipped to Thrive in the Next Decades

What do Agile organizations have in common? Agile organizations are wired for speed, supporting fast decisions, experimentation, learning, empowerment, and cost-effective, cross-functional teamwork, with elements of simplicity, innovation, collaboration, rapid decision-making, knowledge sharing, empowerment, and experimentation. The organizational structure is cross-functional rather than hierarchal, with people, customers, and staff at the center. Since culture is the DNA of any organization, the core values and belief systems become critically important. Using a holistic approach, leaders need to develop processes and structures that will drive the desired results and changes in behaviors (Ho 2020). Once the structure and culture are right, the distribution and execution of work is simplified, integrated, and coordinated.

There are critics of planning and anything "Agile." There have been articles in *The New York Times* and *Forbes*, with headlines announcing: "Strategic planning is dead!" In a recent article in *The Chronicle of Higher Education*, a faculty member was quoted as saying, "Enough with all the harping on 'agility' and 'nimbleness.' Faculty are not dogs—we don't need training" (Utz 2020). Well, this author disagrees with many of the experts as well as many of my faculty colleagues who believe strategic planning is apparently of no value and that Agile is another name for the management "gimmick of the day" that should be ignored and put onto the pile of those already tried and found to be of no use. Despite the cynicism, we all can agree that linear approaches to planning are ineffective as the speed of work and communication increases and new models and approaches are needed. What we can also agree on is that earlier strategic management frameworks and approaches need, at least, to be updated and adapted to this unprecedented time of rapid change and globalization. How do organizations adapt?

By applying Agile principles with good planning practices, including scenarios and automation, and the development of smart teams that seamlessly connect planning and management, organizations will be able to keep tabs on conditions that signal changes ahead and then shift their focus or "Pivot" in response to changed conditions. Management is truly a team game. Leaders who think they can independently scan the environment, match capabilities with opportunities, and build teams capable of exploiting opportunities without input from others are fooling themselves. Think this way and risk being crushed by the steamroller of dynamism and change. I've worked side by side with leaders who believed this and wonder: How many opportunities have been missed? How more could we have done?

In order for Agile organizations to thrive in the next decades, planning and implementation must be inextricably linked. According to a recent study sponsored by the Strategic Implementation Institute, implementation is now viewed for the first time as more important than crafting strategy, but only 28% of the companies surveyed had strategy implementation measurement systems in place, and almost a quarter of the leaders review the implementation progress once a year (Nieto-Rodriguez and Speculand 2020). So, there seems to be a disconnect between what leaders know is needed and how they conduct their businesses. This gap between strategy and execution needs to be paid attention to, requiring leaders who understand the value and invest in it. The combination of vision and execution, of strategy and implementation, has the potential for tremendous upside. Leaders who can be both visionaries and strategies, and are able to modulate between the two, are the ones who can turn their organizations into super competitors (Leinwand and Rotering 2020).

Companies like Starbucks and Apple have mastered the customer experience and put the aesthetic and "feel" of their products front and center. The leaders of those companies, Howard Schultz and Tim Cook, have both visionary and operator skills and deeply value the connection between the two skillsets. In a world where differentiation and uniqueness are highly valued, both require innovative thinking and the development and application of very specific expertise. Developing a bold but executable strategy and then investing in it and bringing along the company to believe in the vision and be willing to execute the plan is the pathway to success with talent, the coin of the realm. Here is how this works:

1. Build a compelling strategy. Include your customers. Be clear about how the firm will add value for the customers in unique ways that build market share.
2. Translate the strategy into the everyday of the firm.

3. Communicate the strategy to everyone, from top to bottom.
4. Create visible programs where everyone is involved.
5. "Advertise progress," letting others know when milestones are met.

Making the Complex, Simple

> *"Simple can be harder than complex: You have to work hard to get your thinking clean to make it simple. But it's worth it in the end because once you get there, you can move mountains."*
> —Steve Jobs

At times, the world seems to simply move too fast, is too complex, and is indecipherable and unknowable. What to do and where your work fits often seems like a complicated question with impossible answers. When managing large organizations and faced with complexity and doubt, I always found solace in this lesson: Everything complex is made up of many simple parts. You need to break down complexity into its smallest units, create priorities, and delegate to staff experts. These are the steps you can follow to begin to manage. Project managers know this lesson well. Here are a few other lessons that may help you.

Permanent Assumptions

> *"Some things are always changing and can't be known. There can also be a handful of things you have unshakable faith in—your permanent assumptions."*
> —Morgan Housel, Collaborative Fund

While trying to synthesize my research, the work of my scholarly and practitioner colleagues, and the constantly emerging, new ideas related to planning and management for the book, I came across an article by Morgan Housel, a partner at the Collaborative Fund and former columnist at *The*

Motley Fool and the *Wall Street Journal*, describing what he calls "Permanent Assumptions," that resonated and related. He said, "How do you analyze the world when everything seems broken? And how do you even begin to make sense of the future when things change so fast? Humbly is the answer" (Housel 2020). A concept often used in investment management circles, permanent assumptions are those handful of things you have "unshakable faith in," things that are always changing and can't be known, or in risk research, the "unknown unknowns." In Housel's example of Amazon, he suggests that there will never be a time when customers would want prices to be higher or deliveries slower. It just would not happen, and so, these are permanent assumptions. Accepting that there are always unknown unknowns is the first step in figuring out how to adapt. As an organization, when you identify and accept these permanent assumptions, you can then focus on shoring up areas of weakness and increasing strategic focus and investment in areas of opportunity.

Why does this matter to planners and executives? When you are identifying opportunities and creating scenarios, prediction, visioning, and prioritizing become important. By being aware of your permanent assumptions, or unknown unknowns, you can focus on what you don't know that, with further research, analysis, and evaluation, can be made sense of. Here are a few of note:

1. The world breaks once a decade. Count on it, and account for it in your industry and your planning.
2. Stories are more powerful than statistics.
3. Nothing too good or bad stays that way forever.
4. History is valuable for understanding how people behave when the world changes.

It is impossible to know what's going to happen in society or the economy, and to some extent, to the climate. What planners need is a reasonable way to account for these variables when building scenarios and visioning an organization's future. Identifying and accounting for the unknown unknowns, or permanent assumptions, provides them with a place to start.

The Strategy of Simple Rules

"Life is really simple, but we insist on making it complicated."
—Confucius

There have been many times over the course of my career where I had to wrestle with a complicated issue involving a number of vendors who were relying on one another, either by design or self-interest, and just couldn't seem to figure out how to work together or where I worked to calm down feuding vice presidents who were being protective of their turf and willing to sabotage peers to get what they want. Despite my best efforts, I couldn't get the opposing teams to cooperate or the combatants to stand down. I am sure these stories are familiar to you. When I began to lose sleep and stress over what seem to be unsolvable, intractable problems, my mind shifted toward simplicity and the overused axiom: "Keep it simple stupid," or Occam's razor, "the simplest solution is usually the right one." Before describing how simplicity can help us cope, let's consider the forces at work, and take a brief look at what the scholars say.

Strategy scholars and organizational theorists have spent a significant amount of research time considering how organizational structure shapes performance in dynamic environments. Studies in this area often highlight a fundamental tension between possessing too little and too much structure, with those organizations using too little structure lacking enough guidance to efficiently generate appropriate behaviors, and those using too much structure becoming too constrained and lacking flexibility. This fundamental tension is a particularly acute dilemma for organizations competing in dynamic environments, as success in these settings demands both efficiency and flexibility. Studies show that high-performing organizations resolve this tension by using a moderate amount of structure, referred to in Agile as soft guide rails, to improvise a variety of innovative solutions. Orton and Weick (1990) noted that loosely coupled units need to be responsive enough to remain coordinated but possess enough separateness to act independently, while other scholars emphasize moderate connectivity among parts of an organization as the optimal way for units to interact. In the Davis, Eisenhardt, and Bingham study (2006), they refer to the tension between too little and too much structure as the "guiding melody" within which organizational improvisation occurs.

In the simple rules strategy, improvisation—referred to in Agile as asymmetry—does not materialize out of thin air but reveals itself as a simple melody (or simple rule) that provides the pretext for real-time composing (Weick 1998). Similarly, Brown and Eisenhardt (1997) find that too many or overly complex rules inhibit product development by constraining the improvisation of innovative solutions, while too few or overly simple rules engender too much chaos to be effective. In contrast, a few simple rules possess the "semi-structure" necessary for effective improvisation. Loosely coupled structures and "simple rules" have been observed among high-performing firms in a variety of dynamic industries (Andersen 2004), which is consistent with other hypotheses that suggest there is a positive relationship between the dynamism of markets and the simplicity and effectiveness of strategy. Since Miner, Bassoff, and Moorman (2001) found that, in many cases, novel outcomes (improvisation) depend critically on having some but not too many problem-solving structures other than what appear in the moment, and that too much structure overly routinizes processes to such an extent that producing innovative outcomes is nearly impossible, these ideas are supportive of many of the chaos-related management challenges and directly and significantly affect how organizations plan.

When applied to organizations, complexity theory seeks to understand how system-level adaptation to the environment emerges from the actions of its agents with a counterintuitive feature that systems composed of a few simple structures give rise to adaptive behavior. By condensing past learning into simple structures, which we have referred to as "simple rules," these systems are able to enjoy a balance of order and disorder that enables adaptation. These rules are simple in two ways: 1) the number of rules should be small, and 2) each rule should be guided by only a few direct actions. Systems balancing order and disorder are adaptive because they are efficient yet not too rigid in their response to change.

The challenge leaders face is to make something that is inherently complex simple so stakeholders and customers understand what you are doing and why. As we work faster and harder to try and keep pace with automation and systems, the cost of complexity increases in financial, social, and personal terms. With organizations almost at a tipping point of human comprehension, it seems more like a survival strategy to boil this increased velocity of work down into simple principles, but it works!

In Julia Hobsbawm's book *The Simplicity Principle*, she suggests leaders can adapt or make sense of complexity by looking at it through two lenses: 1) keeping it simple and 2) learning from nature. Simplicity creates calm and creativity. It brings balance to what is complex, what needs to be unpacked and sorted, and what requires workarounds and adaptation. I am quite sure that striving toward simplicity in all that you do will improve communications, calm down the flittering mind, and help reduce the constant competition for attention from among the most vocal and noisy constituencies. By keeping it simple, the most important work will get done, and the rest will either wait or get attention elsewhere.

When we apply the lessons of nature to our organizations, we begin to rely upon aspects of complexity management, including pattern recognition and the development of intuition. Hobsbawm suggests using the hexagon shape, commonly found in nature, and the so-called "perfect number" in mathematics (six) as the building blocks for simplicity (Hobsbawm 2020a). It is strong as seen in the honeycomb and useful as in the building blocks of the carbon molecule. These simple rules, with simple visualizations, can help leaders, managers, and planners break down complexity into manageable parts, and in doing so, will avoid becoming overwhelmed in their attempts to understand individual interactions and, in the longer term, trying to predict the future.

Agile organizations are structured to help adapt the rules of simplicity by encouraging teamwork, ideation, and expertise sharing. As a result, they are best prepared to understand complex behaviors and changes in their environment. Even so, in this era of complexity, dynamism, disruption, and agility, planners have their hands full. We need to investigate successful firms to understand how they plan and how they cope.

Amazon and Simplicity

> *"In a world filled with complexity,*
> *the basic fundamentals still reign supreme."*
> —Jeff Bezos

Amazon has avoided the natural evolution from Agile start-up to large-scale bureaucracy by bypassing organizational layering, titles, and internal seniority and focusing on building a culture that is "customer first." Their relentless focus on the customer came from the top. It began with a letter to shareholders from Jeff Bezos in 1997 announcing that their Leadership Principle 1 would be "Customer Obsession," an approach that has proven durable and wildly successful. How do they manage this obsession? Amazon uses metrics to drive performance. Amazon doesn't start a new initiative in their planning exercises unless the team has figured out how they will measure the customer's response. Part of this approach to planning and management recognizes that metrics are nearly impossible to retrofit, so they need to be developed, understood, and embedded from the very start.

Customer input is provided from the start, and managers prepare an exhaustive, six-page document explaining the new activity as a narrative that, according to John Rossman, a former Amazon executive, provides for better ideas, more clarity, and better conversation and review. The narrative is supported by a "PR/FAQ" or an imagined press release describing how the customers will be better served by the activity, along with an anticipation of questions likely to be asked. The discipline brought to the process forces the proposer to clearly think through the value of the new activity and the customer's likely interest and acceptance, along with gaining the executive team's acceptance before launching forward (Denning 2020). According to Rossman, once approved, "the narrative documents are incorporated into the annual review process where the merits of every activity and capability, present and future, are evaluated in terms of their contribution and value to the customers" (Rossman 2019).

At Amazon, new activities are reviewed by executives and not middle management. As the work begins, planning documents are updated as information becomes available, with each team reporting to the entirety of senior management and not just their boss, eliminating favoritism and game-playing. Strategy can be a political process left to the chosen few who have the ear of the leader. By not taking strategy into the field and not including the staff and customers in the process, opportunities are missed. Opportunities only revealed themselves by hearing directly from customers and the teams delivering products and services about the work underway and what is needed (Rossman 2019).

One way to break through problems related to a lack of connectivity between the customer and the company is to iterate and continuously evaluate options and opportunities. The organization's executives and customers are often too far from one another and too reliant on messengers pushing and pulling info up and down the org chart. As a result, messages get misunderstood or missed altogether, portfolios get stagnant, potential is squandered, and opportunities wasted, and in extreme cases, organizations fail. Planning and management need to come together, to be a continuous series of directional decisions, evaluations, and analysis—and then adjustments or Pivots!

Agile Isn't Just for Software Developers

Agile isn't just for software development any longer. It is a management strategy that includes all functions and all areas of the enterprise. One positive outcome resulting from the pandemic crisis is the spike in innovation that has been forced on organizations. And what better way to move toward agility than to convene Agile teams to help work through the crisis? Connecting the teams to the various functional areas in an Agile approach to the management of the enterprise is critical to successful implementation. In the Agile management approach, the core business functions, including finance, IT, and marketing, all work seamlessly with the product design teams in a powerful, responsive, and customer-focused way that is destined to accelerate the development and evolution of the entire organization. Whether these innovations and new ways of doing business will remain after the pandemic is over is anyone's guess, but the hope is that organizations operating as Agile businesses with the flexibility, speed, and decision-making skills consistent with core Agile principles will likely thrive, a result that will be nothing short of remarkable (Berez and Rigby 2020).

The Future of Planning

"Simplicity is the ultimate sophistication."
—Leonardo Da Vinci

In both the short and long terms, planners measure certainty and chart action. Better to set your timelines based on "likely to occur" periods of predictable breakthrough innovation and new product development rather than "pie in the sky" longshots. Amy Webb, the founder of the Future Today Institute, suggests there are four distinct categories for planning: 1) tactics, 2) strategy, 3) visions, and 4) systems-level evolution, with the aim of this approach to identify highly probable events for which there is already data and then work outward with each section a strategic approach until you reach systems-level evolution (Webb 2019).

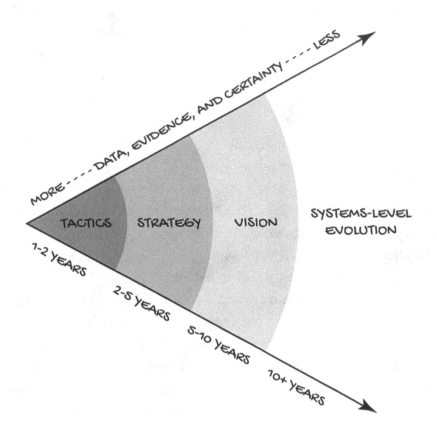

As you can see in the above display, planners can use the edge to consider probability, with the left-hand side representing highly probable events for which there is already data and for which tactics can be developed to get that work underway immediately and then work out from there. Of course, these tactical decisions must fit into the organization's strategy, and when extended into twelve to twenty-four months or beyond, will require defining priorities, allocating resources, and staffing as needed. Other long-term decisions fall into the category of "visions" and need to be planned for, monitored, and considered in future planning exercises (Webb 2019). When thinking about ten or fifteen years into the future, global trends, social changes, and economic shifts need to be part of the vision. These mid to long-term scenarios, along with a description of the future, should be used to guide investments in the long-term in areas such as people and processes. The key is to not get stuck in the tactics and strategy, mission, and vision debates but to accept some level of uncertainty and commit to recalibrating your organization's vision for the future in a regular and systematic way. As you add information and gain experience, the cone becomes more familiar, the variables better understood, and your organization smarter and more resilient.

Webb suggests there are significant technology-based periods ahead, which she calls the "enormous nine," all of which could influence planning, prediction, and decision-making. In a future that includes increasingly intelligent machines with multilayered neural systems, planners could apply this computing power to the multilayers of if-then scenarios involved in prediction. The more data is machined, the more the machine "learns" and is able to refine the output, options, or predictions, and if planning is, in fact, a form of prediction, then we are on to something. Artificial General Insight or AGI, the successor to ANI, the technology that powers Siri and Alexa, will be available at some point in the 2040s with the ability to simulate human qualities at a "ceaselessly stunning pace." How will the thinking and reasoning involved with planning and strategy keep up?

Automation and data machining are the next big steps ahead in strategy and management, with the ability to process, offer options, and implement, adjust, and deploy—at lightning speed. In this new world, how will leaders, planners, and managers decide what to do? What is likely is the much more extensive use of scenarios, designed by smart teams, with data fed into machines to categorize, consider options, calculate probabilities, and predict ranges of success and failure. This AI will build up its very own database or brain, defined as the capacity to consider a world of both autonomous human and non-human information in the way and in the manner it can process and interpret (Webb 2020). Once the machines are finished calculating and providing options, it will be up to people to decide. This vision of the future is not hyperbole and is predicted to take shape over the next decade or two.

Is the Future of Planning, No Planning?

Planning and strategy are headed for a collision with very little distinction between the two. Both are likely to evolve into a process that includes the inputting of data from many different sources and variables (e.g., economic, regulatory, competitive, industry, etc.), along with any changed conditions, fed into a machine that calculates multiple variables and delivers a set of options for the next steps. Teams of "planners" will be responsible for interpreting the output and refining the data sources and analyses to improve the quality and usefulness of the information. While Webb predicts that "AI could be saddled toward elevated, humanistic objectives that have mankind's best advantages at the top of the priority list, such as restoring malignancy or reducing destitution," why not point that capacity toward business and social benefits and competitive advantage? Why not utilize machine learning and superfast systems to outthink, outperform, and outcompete?

For higher education, the future is now. The frivolous debates about the value of planning and the "unique nature of higher ed" are sentiments still being peddled among some faculty, particularly at elite institutions. In the words of Richard Utz, a professor at Georgia Tech, "so dear has the concept become [Agile and agility] that they even demand employees embrace agility" and while comparing faculty to Agile canines, he suggests that once they become "sufficiently Agile, all that's left to do is unleash them on the world" (Utz 2020). This might be humorous if the situation weren't so dire for so many institutions. For higher education, it's time to stop the highbrow frothing and get with it!

Separating the indecision from the decision by taking the time to understand the variables results in the reduction of complexity to simplicity (Hobsbawm 2020). By doing so, communication and collaboration are amplified, resulting in a path to greater teamwork, commitment, and consistency.

Lessons Learned:
- Don't worry about getting within two decimal places of your forecast, but instead, get it directionally right.
- Discourage teams from following a linear decision model. Allow for the development of options or differentiated insights that can result in competitive advantage.
- Plan for serendipity. Challenge teams to return five insights resulting from their work.
- Use the Webb planning cone to guide planning discussions.
- Plan for automation and lightning-fast planning programs.

Challenging Smart Teams to Solve Big Problems

Since Agile management depends largely on smart teams for execution and oversight, how to motivate teams becomes vitally important. Mike Rea suggests tasking teams with a "5X approach," that is, challenging teams to not only develop the drug that solves the current problem but find five other applications for its use. This should be the basis for a new, asymmetric approach to planning, and as the lines between planning and management continue to blur, the way forward for managing. If the future will be based on speed and delivery, planning needs to be continuous and in short increments, with rolling twelve- to twenty-four-month timelines. Smart teams that include members with deep expertise and a strong dose of humility, curiosity, and interest in collaboration are the future.

Leadership Implications

> *"In order to really work effectively, the executive committee, the Agile leadership team, has to work like an Agile team itself."*
> —Darrell Rigby, Bain & Company

In almost all aspects of management, organizations are successful or not because of the leadership, and this is particularly true in this age of Agile. Organizations need leaders willing to admit they don't, and can't, know everything, are willing to coach, ready to guide, and willing to let teams connect with customers and provide answers to problems. Over my career, I have witnessed several examples of leaders jumping into action without fully understanding the situation and imposing weak, flimsy solutions that never take hold and aren't supported by staff, only to fail. Organizations require a leadership strategy that secures and prepares internal leaders for a fast-moving and increasingly volatile and competitive future. As data and communications continue to grow exponentially, it is simply not possible to know everything (Yokoi 2020). Leaders need stronger insights from internal experts and outside the organization to make impactful decisions that maintain liquidity and drive business continuity and performance. Using a connected approach to planning, forecasting, and analysis can help arm them with the added intelligence and greater visibility as they navigate continued volatility (Pichelot 2020).

Agile leadership teams will be made up of people with the right skills, capabilities, and mindsets to play multiple roles (e.g., building and managing the enterprise's operating system, reviewing performance, making adjustments, and figuring out when and how to balance the needs of the central administrative core and the project teams). Operating as a "nerve center" or "control tower," leadership teams need to empower teams within the organization to operate outside of the current bureaucracy by setting up rapid response groups to better deal with shifting priorities.

Alexander, De Smet, Kleinman, and Mugayar-Baldocchi (2020) suggest four steps when building a matrix organization consisting of teams and a coordinating central core:

1. Launch teams fast and build as you go.
2. Get out of the way but stay connected.
3. Champion radical transparency and authenticity.

4. Turbocharge self-organization Many of these steps follow Agile principles and support that approach to teams specifically, and more generally, to Agile management.

Leaders need to be what Yeo (2020) calls "master strategists" who follow these operating behaviors:

1. Ask lots of questions to elevate the quality of discussions and thinking.
2. Welcome the opinions of key stakeholders.
3. Be a great storyteller, engage, and inspire with a compelling vision.

Tomoko Yokoi (2020) suggests that there are specific leadership competencies that relate to an increasingly Agile approach and, ultimately, sustainable success in this era of Agile leadership:

1. **Humility**—Embrace the opportunity to learn and incorporate the ideas of others into problem-solving and solution discussions.
2. **Adaptable**—Be open to new ideas, even when egos may be hurt.
3. **Visionary**—Have a clear sense of long-term direction, even in the face of short-term uncertainty.
4. **Engaged**—Stay engaged and keep your teams engaged.

The good news is that leaders can hone these skills with deliberate and consistent actions and the gaining of experience. They need to keep in mind that in a 2018 Gallup employee satisfaction survey, it found the four primary needs of employees are trust, compassion, stability, and hope. So, the question remains: How do leaders satisfy employee needs, stay engaged, and stay on top of rapidly changing conditions simultaneously? The Agile approach to management is a step in the right direction. However, if a company wants to be fast on its feet and consistently outperform the competition, it needs more than Agile teams; it needs a C-Suite that embraces Agile principles as well (Rigby, Elk, and Berez 2020). Leaders should spend time mentoring, coaching, and deciding, and less time managing subordinates, more time with customers and coaching Agile teams (Denning 2020b).

"Rather than predict the unpredictable,
Agile leaders build rapid feedback loops."
—Darrell Rigby, Sarah Elk, and Steve Berez, Bain & Company

The leaders who took the organization into the pandemic crisis may not be the right ones to lead the organization out of it. The Forbes Insights report (2017), a survey of over 1,000 C-Level executives from around the globe, suggests that C-Suite buy-in is critical for any Agile transformation to be successful and proposes ways to implement the approach. Of those surveyed, over 81% reported recognizing the increased value of organizational agility, 87% said that the CEO needs to be the biggest proponent of agility, 83% cite the right talent or skills as key to a successful transformation, and 44% have introduced a flatter structure to become more Agile. Clearly, Agile management techniques are valued and are being developed and deployed in organizations around the world.

The Time for Agile Is Now

Like a Venn diagram, twenty-first-century strategy has three basic components, all coming together to create meaning and set direction for organizations. The first is planning. Often maligned in the past, the twenty-first-century version needs to be systematic, open to new ideas or asymmetric learning, and encouraging to those involved with the primary goal of bringing new ideas and insights to the planning table. The second is implementation. Often under- or not valued at all, implementation takes over once you've decided the organization's priorities, opportunities, and where you want to experiment or place small bets. During implementation, ideas generated in the planning process are taken into the field to be tested and evaluated and either invested in or abandoned. The third is measurement. In this open and creative organization, boundaries become thoughtfully designed so as to not become barriers and are integral to what the organization decides to do and how they decide to do it.

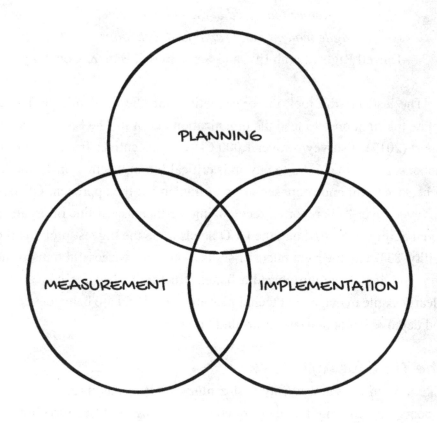

Despite it being widely accepted that organizations need to operate with greater agility, quick iterative cycles, cross-functional teams, and directly with their customers, the challenge for those deploying Agile management principles is the historical operation of rigid and hierarchal structures that are familiar and not conducive to today's modern, digital, networked business forms (Engelmann 2020). So, what do leaders need to do to move forward with an Agile management approach?

First, recognize that the time is now. According to the *Forbes* survey, two-thirds of the organizations have experienced less than 10% revenue growth in the most recent fiscal year, indicating a slowing response to market trends, the need for better products, and not meeting customer expectations.

Second, recognize that every function in your organization can be Agile.

Third, hiring the right mix of talent has never been more important. Leaders need to create an Agile culture by pushing Agile into every corner of the organization.

Fourth, think Agile in all you do. Make it how your business will run.

Fifth, hire the best people and get out of the way. In recent discussions related to higher education leadership, it has been noted that senior leaders need to increasingly rely on staff to develop and execute the necessary solutions in response to the pandemic. They need to decide whether to apply top-down control in its current form, if control can be shared more broadly and where and when they can delegate. As the problems and solutions multiply, reliance on staff will increase in frequency and importance. The bottom line is that leaders will need to observe, evaluate, and make decisions quickly, and while doing so, evaluate which changes are productive and could be adopted in the longer term and which should be discontinued (Sharpe 2020).

According to a recent survey by Korn Ferry, Agile leaders have three key qualities: openness, authentic listening, and adaptability, and above all, they must be able to navigate through ambiguity by creating clarity for their teams. Get the right people in the right positions to make the best decisions, much more like an ecosystem or a biologic system and less like a stiff and structured bureaucracy; get the roles, decision-making, and talent right; get the organizational structure right; get the systems and processes in alignment; and, put the customer front and center.

What all organizations hope for are great ideas that generate business and drive success, however that is measured. Sometimes great ideas happen because of brilliance. Other times someone will see an opportunity and the organization seizes it. Sometimes things happen by coincidence or just dumb luck. The Agile management process is ready for these serendipitous events and designed to generate new ideas with the hope of uncovering the next Amazon, Microsoft, or Johnson & Johnson. In order to create a fertile idea generation culture, staff, leaders, and customers need to work closely together, exposing weaknesses and openly sharing problems followed by unique, efficient, and permanent solutions that become next-generation products and services. A win-win formula.

Final Thoughts

During the COVID pandemic of 2020, teams of researchers and manufacturers worked together like never before. Designing and building ventilators, which generally took a year or more to design and manufacture, were designed, built, and delivered within a month. A global sprint by pharmaceutical companies to develop a vaccine has brought together research teams to share developments and information related to the development, manufacture, and shipment of a vaccine by the end of 2020. A typical drug trial timeline is measured in years, not months. This current cycle is believed to be on track for a start-to-finish development to delivery cycle of six to nine months, lightning speed in the pharmaceutical industry. Why does it take a crisis to realize maximum efficiency? What effect will this pandemic experience have on how organizations function in the future?

Certainly, Agile approaches will become the rule and not the exception. Organizations will need to be more externally focused on developing products and solutions needed by their customers. Smart, multidisciplinary teams and continuous training will become increasingly commonplace as organizations fight for competitive advantage. The "we will build what we think is cool and people will buy" is a sentiment of the past. Competitive pressure, hopefully not due to another crisis but rather as a response to customer need, will result in better, more efficient products and services. Agile avoids making perfection the enemy of "good enough" by getting useful products into the hands of the users, getting feedback, and then generating incremental improvements (Mutlow 2020).

According to McKinsey, the pandemic has dramatically widened the gap between companies at the top and bottom of the power curve of economic profit, the winners and losers in the global corporate performance race. Their research suggests industries that started at the top of the curve before the crisis are proving to be resilient, while those at the bottom are accruing the biggest losses (Bradley et al. 2020). I believe you would find the same trend in higher education, with those at the top of the curve before the pandemic being more resilient and those at the bottom—the tuition-dependent, mid-ranked small to midsize institutions—accruing the biggest losses. Could it be that, as my dissertation found, those with enough money to plan, in any form, outperform the rest (Starsia 2010)? What will be the effect in the corporate sector? Will higher education shake off its history of intransigence and move purposefully into management modernity? Only time will tell.

Many organizations have some experience with the techniques discussed in this book, some due to an interest in improving performance and others applying Agile in isolated instances and due to a situational imperative. I am confident that management is changing quickly and profoundly. This is not a situation to be tolerated but rather a moment, accelerated by a crisis, that is forcing all organizations to assess their capacity and capabilities. Leaders need to put all the tools and techniques in place and recruit the smartest and most experienced staff available to deploy strategy in one continuous process, making that approach part of the organization's working habits and culture. The engine undergirding this approach includes informed, cooperative planning and product management teams who focus on the next opportunity to leverage capabilities, prepare for inevitable change, and be ready to take advantage when the tides of disruption come ashore.

"Having one fast, Agile team is helpful, but having many of them across an enterprise, and enabling them with the right structures, processes, and culture, makes it possible for the entire system to move faster."
—McKinsey & Company

It seems like we humans are hitting a plateau where the flow of information is so fast and so ubiquitous as to make decision-making difficult and more intuitive than structured. Decision makers can become easily overwhelmed. In a 2020 study, McKinsey & Company suggests the "need for speed" and that there's no turning back. Organizations designed for speed will see powerful outcomes (e.g., greater customer responsiveness, enhanced capabilities, and better performance), increased efficiencies, and a return on capital (De Smet, Pacthod, Relyea, and Sternfels 2020). Will the future of planning and strategy include the use of emerging technologies such as neural networks, brain mapping, virtual and augmented reality, generative systems, superhuman insight, and simulated and advanced artificial intelligence?

A planning and strategic implementation process that highlights asymmetric learning, rather than prescriptive outcomes, is a new way to think about strategic thinking and planning. While I'm not quite ready to make the leap to relying exclusively on the list of emerging technologies mentioned earlier, I do think that more automation is better than less, that more historical data collection and analysis will improve planning, that a deep commitment to continuous planning and learning (characteristics of Agile management) needs to be made, and that more learning and sharing and scenario development will inform decisions and create a competitive advantage. I am quite confident that organizations not following a continuous planning and management process will find themselves outside looking in, and those organizations investing in continuous planning and smart strategies and building a strategic culture will outperform those doing less.

So, Where Do We Go from Here?

There are resources available for those interested in learning more about planning and implementation:

- Gartner's 2019 Market Guide for Strategy Execution Management Software report lists more than twenty companies specializing in Strategic Execution Management (SEM) software platforms

- IDEA Pharma blog for leading-edge ideas related to asymmetric learning
- Strategic Implementation Institute at https://www.strategyimplementationinstitute.org
- Strategic Planning for Nonprofits at https://www.councilofnonprofits.org/tools-resources

There is no doubt that organizations of all types have to incorporate technological advances into a formalized planning approach. Using technologies to visualize potential and possible futures is proving to be useful in the collection of planning-related data that will fuel smart teams to build some aspects of strategy and planning into their day-to-day work. Teams must look ahead and prepare for a future likely to include more and faster change. They need to develop expertise to operate increasingly sophisticated technologies to help collect, analyze, and share data that explains where the organization is going in the short term, along with visualized possible future states.

During a trip to Shanghai Jiao Tong University in Shanghai, China, in 2008, I met with an SJTU colleague, Nian Liu, a professor in their School of Management and the university's strategic planning department leader. Professor Liu was also the founder of the World Rankings of Colleges and Universities, the first attempt at comparing institutions on a global level. I asked him how they create strategy and plan. To my surprise, he shared that SJTU had a department staffed by faculty, graduate students, and statisticians thoroughly familiar with the global higher-education industry. It is worth noting that, at that time, the institution I was working at had no strategic plan, no strategic planning department, and no one working on a plan. Fortunately, the new president added a cabinet-level strategy leader on the executive team, and for the first time, planning was included in leadership discussions. Because the team had some experience creating a plan and new strategies, this proved critical when the pandemic hit, and plans became fluid and super flexible.

Perhaps elite institutions with large endowments, a history of fund-raising success, and a cadre of dedicated alumni can afford to be slow to strategic planning and Agility. Perhaps the riches found at elite universities will delay the need for dedicated resources to strategic planning and Agile management. My take? This may be true in the short run, but as an increasing number of elite public institutions grow both residential programs and online enrollments, those in the middle to lower tier and the small institutions with little endowment—all battling for increasingly scarce resources—will have to figure out a niche and a strategic plan that maps out a path to future success.

For corporate leaders, what does the future look like with an ever-expanding Amazon driving into more and more industries, gobbling up market share and redefining markets? How will electric vehicles change the automobile, oil and gas, and infrastructure industries? Disruption is well underway across industries and around the globe. Identify your niche. Hire smart people. Pilot new ideas. Measure progress… and Plan to Pivot.

ABOUT THE AUTHOR

Gerry Starsia has enjoyed a unique career as a practitioner, business owner, and operator, followed by a pivot to higher education as an executive, academic, and author. Over the last two decades, he has been on the faculty at the University of Virginia with split roles that include teaching undergraduate, graduate, and executive classes and as Senior Associate Dean and Chief Operating Officer at the McIntire School of Commerce and the Darden Graduate School of Business. Prior to his tenure at UVA, Gerry was the Founder/CEO of a medical design-build firm.

He serves on several for-profit and nonprofit boards of directors, consults with many small to mid-size start-up and growth firms and nonprofits, and advises a number of executives and entrepreneurs.

Gerry lives in Charlottesville, Virginia, with his wife, Marianne.

Learn more at GerryStarsia.com.

REFERENCES

Agile Center 2020: "The Benefits of Adopting the SAFe Framework for Your Team." Agile Center. https://agile-center.com/blog/87-the-bene-fits-of-adopting-the-safe-framework-for-your-team.html.

Agile Center 2020a: "SAFe Devops: The Great Opportunities of Integrating Devops and Agile." Agile Center. https://agile-center.com/blog/120-safe-devops-the-great-opportunities-of-integrating-devops-and-agile.html.

Agile Strategy Manager 2020: "Agile Strategy Framework: Agile Strategy Execution Framework." https://www.agilestrategymanager.com/strategy-framework.html.

Alexander, De Smet, Kleinman, and Mugayar-Baldocchi 2020: Alexander, Andrea, Aaron De Smet, Sarah Kleinman, and Marino Mugayar-Baldocchi. "To Weather a Crisis, Build a Network of Teams." McKinsey & Company, July 22, 2020. https://www.mckinsey.com/business-functions/organization/our-insights/to-weather-a-crisis-build-a-network-of-teams.

Andersen 2004: Andersen, Torben Juul. "Integrating Decentralized Strategy Making and Strategic Planning Processes in Dynamic Environments." Wiley Online Library. John Wiley & Sons, Ltd, November

26, 2004. https://onlinelibrary.wiley.com/doi/10.1111/j.1467-6486.2004.00475.x.

Bacon 2020: Bacon, James. "An Intellectual-Diversity Agenda for UVa." Bacons Rebellion. https://www.baconsrebellion.com/wp/an-intellectual-diversity-agenda-for-uva/.

Baldwin 2020: Baldwin, Roberto. "China's CATL Has a Million-Mile EV Battery Pack Ready to Go." *Car and Driver*, November 10, 2020. https://www.caranddriver.com/news/a32801823/million-mile-ev-battery-pack-revealed/.

Berez and Rigby 2020: Berez, Steve, and Darrell Rigby. "How Agile Can Future-Proof Your Organization." The Enterprisers Project, June 19, 2020. https://enterprisersproject.com/article/2020/6/agile-how-future-proof.

Blank 2010: Blank, Steve. "Why Startups Are Agile and Opportunistic—Pivoting the Business Model." April 12, 2010. https://steveblank.com/2010/04/12/why-startups-are-Agile-and-opportunistic-%E2%80%93-Pivoting-the-business-model/.

Bradley, Hirt, Hudson, Northcote, and Smit 2020: Bradley, Chris, Martin Hirt, Sara Hudson, Nicholas Northcote, and Sven Smit. "The Great Acceleration." McKinsey & Company, December 14, 2020. https://www.mckinsey.com/business-functions/strategy-and-corporate-finance/our-insights/the-great-acceleration.

Bryson 2018: Bryson, John. *Strategic Planning for Public and Nonprofit Organizations*. Hoboken, NJ: John Wiley & Sons, 2018.

Bryson and Finn 1995: Halachmi, Arie, and Geert Bouckaert. *The Enduring Challenges in Public Management: Surviving and Excelling in a Changing World*, 247–80. "Creating the Future Together: Developing and Using Shared Strategy Maps"—John M. Bryson and Charles B. Finn. San Francisco: Jossey-Bass Publishers, 1995.

Bungay 2019: Bungay, Stephen. "5 Myths About Strategy." *Harvard Business Review*, April 22, 2019. https://hbr.org/2019/04/5-myths-about-strategy.

Business Agility Institute 2019: Leybourn, Evan. "2019 Business Agility Report: Raising the BAR." Business Agility Institute, August 6, 2019. https://businessagility.institute/learn/2019-business-agility-report-raising-the-bar/243.

Business Matters 2020: "How a Low-Code Platform Empowers an Agile Leader to Achieve Enterprise Agility." *Business Matters*, May 20, 2020. https://bmmagazine.co.uk/business/how-a-low-code-platform-empowers-an-agile-leader-to-achieve-enterprise-agility/.

Carey 2020: Carey, Benedict. "Can an Algorithm Predict the Pandemic's Next Moves?" *The New York Times*, July 2, 2020. https://www.nytimes.com/2020/07/02/health/santillana-coronavirus-model-forecast.html.

Charumilind, El Turabi, Finn, and Usher 2020: Charumilind, Sarun, Anas El Turabi, Patrick Finn, and Ophelia Usher. "Demystifying Modeling: How Quantitative Models Can—and Can't—Explain the World." McKinsey & Company, July 16, 2020. https://www.mckinsey.com/business-functions/risk/our-insights/demystifying-modeling-how-quantitative-models-can-and-cant-explain-the-world.

Collaborative Strategy 2020a: "Pivoting—The Essential Capability of an Agile Business." Collaborative Strategy. https://www.collaborativestrategy.ca/Pivoting-the-essential-capability-of-an-Agile-business/.

Collaborative Strategy 2020b: "Saving Strategy—How to Make 'Doing Strategy' Meaningful in an Age of Disruption." Collaborative Strategy. https://www.collaborativestrategy.ca/saving-strategy-make-strategy-meaningful-age-disruption/.

Comella-Dorda, Handscomb, and Zaidi 2020: Comella-Dorda, Santiago, Christopher Handscomb, and Ahmad Zaidi. "Agility to Action: Operationalizing a Value-Driven Agile Blueprint." McKinsey & Company, June 16, 2020. https://www.mckinsey.com/business-functions/organization/our-insights/agility-to-action-operationalizing-a-value-driven-agile-blueprint.

ContinuityCentral.com 2020: "Agile Leadership Will Be One of the Keys to Help Organizations Adapt to the New Normal." https://www.continuitycentral.com/index.php/news/resilience-news/5314-agile-leadership-will-be-one-of-the-keys-to-help-organizations-adapt-to-the-new-normal.

Cowan 2020: Cowan, Alex. "Agile Development." Coursera. https://www.coursera.org/specializations/agile-development.

Dalio 2019: Davis, Owen. "Ray Dalio Thinks the Media Should Be Less Sensationalistic about How Sensational Ray Dalio Is." Dealbreaker, January 3, 2017. https://dealbreaker.com/2017/01/ray-dalio-media-critic.

D'Auria, Dotiwala, and Gast 2020: D'Auria, Gemma, Faridun Dotiwala, and Arne Gast. "Sustainably Shifting How an Organization Leads." McKinsey & Company. https://www.mckinsey.com/business-functions/organization/our-insights/the-organization-blog/sustainably-shifting-how-an-organization-leads.

Davis 2020: Interview with Jonathan Davis, CEO, Martha Jefferson Hospital. June 10, 2020.

Denning 2020: Denning, Steve. "Understanding What Good Agile Looks Like." *Forbes*, August 14, 2020. *Table: The Principles, Processes and Practices of Agile vs. 20th Century Management*. https://www.forbes.com/sites/stevedenning/2020/08/09/understanding-what-good-agile-looks-like/.

Denning 2020a: Denning, Steve. "How Amazon Became Agile." *Forbes*, June 30, 2021. https://www.forbes.com/sites/stevedenning/2019/06/02/how-amazon-became-agile/.

Denning 2020b: Denning, Steve. "Why Only the Agile Will Survive." *Forbes*, April 19, 2020. https://www.forbes.com/sites/stevedenning/2020/04/19/why-only-the-agile-will-survive/.

Denning 2020c: Denning, Steve. "Explaining Agile." *Forbes*, June 30, 2021. https://www.forbes.com/sites/stevedenning/2016/09/08/explaining-agile/.

De Smet, Pacthod, Relyea, and Sternfels 2020: De Smet, Aaron, Daniel Pacthod, Charlotte Relyea, and Bob Sternfels. "Ready, Set, Go: Reinventing the Organization for Speed in the Post-COVID-19 Era." McKinsey & Company, March 10, 2021. https://www.mckinsey.com/business-functions/organization/our-insights/ready-set-go-reinventing-the-organization-for-speed-in-the-post-covid-19-era.

Dimon 2019: Son, Hugh. "JP Morgan Is Rolling out the First US Bank-Backed Cryptocurrency to Transform Payments Business." CNBC, February 15, 2019. https://www.cnbc.com/2019/02/13/jp-morgan-is-rolling-out-the-first-us-bank-backed-cryptocurrency-to-transform-payments--.html.

Duggal 2018: Duggal, Jack. *The DNA of Strategy Execution*. Hoboken, NJ: John Wiley & Sons, 2018.

Engelmann 2020: Engelmann, Eric. "The Elusive Agile Enterprise: How the Right Leadership Mindset, Workforce and Culture Can Transform Your Organization." Forbes Insights and Scrum Alliance, n.d. https://resources.scrumalliance.org/Article/elusive-agile-enterprise-forbes-insights-report.

Exhibit 1a: Scenario Planning—Visioning Endstates. "Future Mapping." Anthros Consulting. http://www.anthrosconsulting.com/future-mapping.

Exhibit 1b: Scenario Planning—Framework to Monitor Progress. "Future Mapping." Anthros Consulting. http://www.anthrosconsulting.com/future-mapping.

Exhibit 2a: "Scenario Planning—Visioning Endstates." ADK Futures Project. http://www.adkfutures.net/EndState.

Exhibit 2b: "Scenario Planning—Visioning Endstates Description." ADK Futures: Endstate. http://www.adkfutures.net/EndState/Detail/1.

Exhibit 2c: "Scenario Planning—Ranking Endstates by Desirability & Attainability Summary." ADK Futures: The Future. http://www.adkfutures.net/TheFuture.

Exhibit 2d: "Scenario Planning—Ranking Endstates by Desirability & Attainability." ADK Futures: Ranking Results. http://www.adkfutures. net/Ranking.

Exhibit 3: "Scenario Planning—Endstates Synthesis." ADK Futures: Endstate Synthesis. http://www.adkfutures.net/TheFuture/Synthesis.

Fainshmidt, Wenger, Pezeshkan, and Mallon 2019: Fainshmidt, Stav, Lucas Wenger, Amir Pezeshkan, and Mark Mallon. "When Do Dynamic Capabilities Lead to Competitive Advantage? The Importance of Strategic Fit." *Journal of Management Studies* 56:4, June 2019. P. 758-787. John Wiley & Sons, December 10, 2018. https:// onlinelibrary.wiley.com/doi/abs/10.1111/joms.12415.

Ferrazzi 2020: Ferrazzi, Keith. "How Agile Is Helping Unilever Go Forward Faster." *Forbes*, July 10, 2020. https://www.forbes.com/sites/ keithferrazzi/2020/06/17/how-agile-is-helping-unilever-go-forward-faster/.

Frey and Osborne 2013: Frey, Carl, and Michael Osborne. "The Future of Employment: How Susceptible Are Jobs to Computerisation?" Oxford Martin Programme on Technology and Employment, September 17, 2013. https://www.oxfordmartin.ox.ac.uk/publications/the-future-of-employment/.

Friga 2020a: Friga, Paul. "Under COVID-19, University Budgets Like We've Never Seen Before." *The Chronicle of Higher Education*, July 23, 2020. https://www.chronicle.com/article/under-covid-19-university-budgets-like-weve-never-seen-before/.

Friga 2020b: Friga, Paul. "Will College Athletics Survive? Should They?" *The Chronicle of Higher Education*, July 23, 2020. https:// www.chronicle.com/article/will-college-athletics-survive-should-they.

Gabbatis 2020: Gabbatis, Josh. "Can the Wood-Wide Web Really Help Trees Talk to Each Other?" *BBC Science Focus Magazine*, May 15, 2020. https://www.sciencefocus.com/nature/mycorrhizal-networks-wood-wide-web/.

Gard 2020: Gard, Richard. "From Vax to Stacks." *Virginia Magazine.* https://uvamagazine.org/articles/from_the_editor_winter_2020.

Gardner 2020: Gardner, Lee. "Why Colleges' Plans for Fall Are Like 'Nailing Jell-O to the Wall.'" *The Chronicle of Higher Education,* July 22, 2020. https://www.chronicle.com/article/why-colleges-plans-for-fall-are-like-nailing-jell-o-to-the-wall.

Gates and Hemingway 2009: Gates, Bill, and Collins Hemingway. *Business @ the Speed of Thought: Succeeding in the Digital Economy.* New York: Grand Central Publishing, 2009.

Gawande 2011: Gawande, Atul. "Cowboys and Pit Crews." *The New Yorker,* May 26, 2011. https://www.newyorker.com/news/news-desk/cowboys-and-pit-crews.

Girvan 2020: Girvan, Simon. "The Uncomfortable Truth about Agile." BCS. https://www.bcs.org/content-hub/the-uncomfortable-truth-about-agile/.

Global Sport Matters 2018: "Athletes Are Right: The Game Really Does Slow Down for Them." Global Sport Matters, May 16, 2018. https://globalsportmatters.com/science/2018/05/16/athletes-are-right-the-game-really-does-slow-down-for-them/.

Grube, Polyakov, and Röder 2021: Grube, Christian, Yuri Polyakov, and Tido Röder. "Scenario-Based Cash Planning in a Crisis: Lessons for the Next Normal." McKinsey & Company, January 21, 2021. https://www.mckinsey.com/business-functions/strategy-and-corporate-finance/our-insights/scenario-based-cash-planning-in-a-crisis-lessons-for-the-next-normal.

Hadaya and Gagnon 2020: Hadaya, Pierre, and Bernard Gagnon. "Mapping an Agile Future." *Strategy Magazine,* Issue #35, 2020.

Haden 2013: Interview with James Haden, CEO, Martha Jefferson Hospital. June 12, 2012.

Haden and Cottrell 2013b: Interview with James Haden, CEO, and Ron Cottrell, Vice President, Martha Jefferson Hospital. July 7, 2013.

Hambrick and Fredrickson 2001: Hambrick, Donald, and James Fredrickson. "Are You Sure You Have a Strategy?" *Academy of Management Perspectives*. Vol. 15, No. 4., November 1, 2005. https://journals.aom.org/doi/abs/10.5465/ame.2005.19417907.

Hardesty 2017: Hardesty, Larry. "Researchers Add a Splash of Human Intuition to Planning Algorithms." MIT News | Massachusetts Institute of Technology. MIT Computer Science & Artificial Intelligence Lab, Feb. 7, 2017. https://news.mit.edu/2017/human-intuition-planning-algorithms-0207.

Haynes 2020: Haynes, Felix. "COLUMN: Agile Non-Profits Pivot to Meet New Pandemic Needs." *Plant City Observer*, May 20, 2020. https://www.plantcityobserver.com/column-agile-non-profits-pivot-to-meet-new-pandemic-needs/.

Hill 2019: Hill, Andrew. "Artificial Intelligence Creates Real Strategic Dilemmas." *Financial Times*, May 20, 2019. https://www.ft.com/content/8e3d9386-77c6-11e9-bbad-7c18c0ea0201.

Ho 2020: Ho, Irlana. "The Power of Agility: Pivoting and Thriving in a Time of Uncertainty." Culture Pivot Solutions, April 7, 2020. https://www.culturepivotsolutions.com/power-of-agility-Pivoting-in-a-time-of-covid19-pandemic/.

Hobsbawm 2020: Hobsbawm, Julia. *The Simplicity Principle: Six Steps Towards Clarity in a Complex World*. London, UK: Kogan Page, 2020.

Hobsbawm 2020a: Hobsbawm, Julia. "The Simplicity Principle and Why Six Is the Perfect Number for Better Management." Strategy+Business, April 28, 2020. https://www.strategy-business.com/article/The-Simplicity-Principle-and-why-six-is-the-perfect-number-for-better-management.

Horrigan 2020: Horrigan, Mia. "Rapid Pivoting and Responsiveness Will Be the 'New Normal.'" Zen Ex Machina, May 5, 2021. https://zenex-machina.com/rapid-Pivoting-and-responsiveness-is-the-new-normal/.

Housel 2020: Housel, Morgan. "Permanent Assumptions." Collaborative Fund, June 4, 2020. https://www.collaborativefund.com/blog/permanent-assumptions/.

Kaplan 2020: Kaplan, Sarah. "What It Means for Businesses to 'Build Back Better' after COVID-19." *Fast Company*, May 13, 2020. https://www.fastcompany.com/90504151/what-it-means-for-businesses-to-build-back-better-after-covid-19.

Kaplan 2012: Kaplan, Soren. "4 Innovation Strategies from Big Companies That Act like Startups." *Fast Company*, October 10, 2012. https://www.fastcompany.com/1670960/4-innovation-strategies-from-big-companies-that-act-like-startups.

Kay and King 2020: Kay, John, and Mervyn King. *Radical Uncertainty: Decision-Making Beyond the Numbers*. W.W. Norton & Company, 2020.

Kenny 2016: Kenny, Graham. "Strategic Plans Are Less Important than Strategic Planning." *Harvard Business Review*, June 21, 2016. https://hbr.org/2016/06/strategic-plans-are-less-important-than-strategic-planning.

Knight 2020: Knight, Cassidy. "Agile Done, Done Done, or Pivot?" Cprime, August 10, 2019. https://www.cprime.com/resources/blog/Agile-done-done-done-or-Pivot/.

Koppensteiner and Udo 2009: Koppensteiner, Sonja, and Nathalie Udo. "An Agile Guide to the Planning Processes." Paper presented at PMIâ Global Congress 2009—EMEA, Amsterdam, North Holland, The Netherlands: Newtown Square, PA: Project Management Institute, May 20, 2009.

Leinwand and Rotering 2020: Leinwand, Paul, and Joachim Rotering. "How to Excel at Both Strategy and Execution." *Harvard Business Review*, January 17, 2019. https://hbr.org/2017/11/how-to-excel-at-both-strategy-and-execution.

Leinwand and Mainardi 2016: Leinwand, Paul, and Cesare Mainardi. *Strategy That Works: How Winning Companies Close the Strategy-to-Execution Gap*. Boston, MA: Harvard Business Review Press, 2016.

Lewis 2021: Lewis, Michael. *The Premonition: A Pandemic Story*. New York: W.W. Norton & Company, 2021.

Markides 2008: Markides, Constantinos. *Game-Changing Strategies: How to Create New Market Space in Established Industries by Breaking the Rules*. San Francisco, CA: Jossey-Bass, 2008.

Martin 2014: Martin, Roger. "The Big Lie of Strategic Planning." *Harvard Business Review*, January–February 2014. https://hbr. org/2014/01/the-big-lie-of-strategic-planning.

Martinez and Wolverton 2009: Martinez, Mario, and Mimi Wolverton. *Innovative Strategy Making in Higher Education*. Charlotte, NC: Information Age Publishing, 2009.

McPhee 1978: McPhee, John. *A Sense of Where You Are*. New York: Farrar, Straus, and Giroux, 1978.

Miller 2003: Miller, Danny. "An Asymmetry-Based View of Advantage: Towards an Attainable Sustainability." *Strategic Management Journal*, Volume 24, Issue 10. September 12, 2003. https://www.jstor.org/ stable/20060591.

Miner, Bassoff, and Moorman 2001: Miner, Anne, Paula Bassoff, and Christine Moorman. "Organizational Improvisation and Learning: A Field Study." *Administrative Science Quarterly*, 46: 304–337, 2001.

Mintzberg 1994: Mintzberg, Henry. "The Fall and Rise of Strategic Planning." *Harvard Business Review*, January–February 1994. https://hbr. org/1994/01/the-fall-and-rise-of-strategic-planning.

Mitchell 2012: Interview with John Mitchell, CEO, IPC. June 5, 2012.

Mutlow 2020: Mutlow, Nerys. "How to Turn Chaos into Competitive Advantage." *Forbes*, May 15, 2020. https://www.forbes.com/sites/servicenow/2020/05/15/how-to-turn-chaos-into-competitive-advantage/.

Nakano 2012: Nakano, C. "Agile Business: Demystifying the Pivot." MindManager, June 28, 2012. https://blog.mindmanager.com/ blog/2012/06/Agile-business-demystifying-the-Pivot/.

O'Reilly and Tushman 2008: O'Reilly, Charles, and Michael Tushman. "Ambidexterity as a Dynamic Capability: Resolving the Innovator's

Dilemma." Research in Organizational Behavior, 28, 185–296, June 30, 2008. https://www.sciencedirect.com/science/article/abs/pii/S0191308508000105.

Parker and Stacey 1994: Parker, David, and Ralph D. Stacey. *Chaos, Management and Economics*. London: Institute of Economic Affairs, 1994.

Peters 2020: Peters, Adele. "This 22-Foot Long 'Problem Map' Looks at the Systemic Failures That Made COVID Spread in the U.S." *Fast Company*, June 17, 2020. https://www.fastcompany.com/90517512/this-22-foot-long-problem-map-looks-at-the-systemic-failures-that-made-covid-spread-in-the-u-s.

Pichelot 2020: Pichelot, Nadine. "Data-Driven Planning Helps Businesses Remain Agile." *Bobs Guide*, May 26, 2020. https://www.bobsguide.com/articles/data-driven-planning-helps-businesses-remain-agile/.

Project Management Institute 2018: "Success in Disruptive Times." https://www.pmi.org/-/media/pmi/documents/public/pdf/learning/thought-leadership/pulse/pulse-of-the-profession-2018.pdf.

Pusser 2008: Recollections of a conversation with Buford Pusser.

PwC 2017: "20 Years inside the Mind of the CEO… What's Next?" 20th CEO Survey. https://www.pwc.com/gx/en/ceo-survey/2017/pwc-ceo-20th-survey-report-2017.pdf.

Rea 2020a: Rea, Mike. "Asymmetric Learning—The New Competitive Advantage." https://www.linkedin.com/pulse/asymmetric-learning-new-competitive-advantage-mike-rea/.

Rea 2020b: Interview with Mike Rea, CEO, IDEA Pharma. June 24, 2020.

Rice 2012: Rice, Andrew. "Anatomy of a Campus Coup." *The New York Times*, September 11, 2012. https://www.nytimes.com/2012/09/16/magazine/teresa-sullivan-uva-ouster.html.

Ries 2012: Ries, Eric. "Eric Ries Explains the Pivot," Presentation at SXSW, October 19, 2012. https://www.youtube.com/watch?v=1hTl4z2ijc4.

Rigby, Elk, and Berez 2020: Rigby, Darrell, Sarah Elk, and Steve Berez. "The Agile C-Suite." *Harvard Business Review*, May–June 2020. https://hbr.org/2020/05/the-agile-c-suite.

Ringland and Young 2006: Ringland, Gill, and Laurie Young. "A History of Scenarios." John Wiley & Sons. https://onlinelibrary.wiley.com/doi/pdf/10.1002/9780470666265.app3.

Robinson 2020: Robinson, Murray. "Agile Initiative Planning with Roadmaps." *InfoQ*, July 9, 2020. https://www.infoq.com/articles/agile-initiative-planning/.

Romo 2013: Pompei, Dan. "Dallas Cowboys Quarterback Tony Romo Getting Better with Age." *Bleacher Report*, December 6, 2013. https://bleacherreport.com/articles/1878186-cowboys-quarterback-tony-romo-getting-better-with-age.

Rossman 2019: Rossman, John. *Think like Amazon: 50 1/2 Ideas to Become a Digital Leader*. New York: McGraw-Hill Education, 2019.

Rouse 2016: Rouse, William. *Universities as Complex Enterprises*. Hoboken, NJ: John Wiley & Son, 2016.

Salisbury 2019: Salisbury, Allison Dulin. "New Higher-Ed Business Models That Millions of Americans Need to Get Better Jobs." *EdSurge News*, April 1, 2019. https://www.edsurge.com/news/2019-04-01-new-higher-ed-business-models-millions-of-americans-need-to-get-better-jobs.

SD Learning Consortium 2017: "2017 Report of the SD Learning Consortium." https://sdlearningconsortium.com/.

Sharpe 2020: Sharpe, Richard. "Leading and Learning through Uncertainty." *University World News,* July 12, 2020. https://www.universityworldnews.com/post.php?story=20200708171028609.

Sherrington 2020a: Interview with Gemma Sherrington, Executive Director of Fundraising and Marketing, Save the Children. June 9, 2020.

Sherrington 2020b: Sherrington, Gemma. "Agile Transformation: Save the Children's Fundraising Lead on Its New Operating Model." *Fundraising Magazine*, May 11, 2020. https://www.civilsociety.

co.uk/fundraising/agile-transformation-save-the-children-new-operating-model.html.

Sickafus 2001: Sickafus, Edward. *Unified Structured Inventive Thinking: An Overview*. Grosse Ile, MI: NTELLECK, 1997. https://edsickafus.files.wordpress.com/2015/08/eusit1enver2.pdf.

Stang and Handler 2019: Stang, Daniel, and Robert Handler. "Market Guide for Strategy Execution Management Software." Gartner Research, November 25, 2019. https://www.gartner.com/en/documents/3975499/market-guide-for-strategy-execution-management-software.

Starsia 2010: "Strategic Planning in Higher Education: An Examination of Variation in Strategic Planning Practices and Their Effect on Success in NCAA Division I Athletic Departments." https://eric.ed.gov/?id=ED523626.

Statista 2021: "Percentage of Students in the United States Taking Distance Learning Courses from 2012 to 2019." Statista. https://www.statista.com/statistics/944245/student-distance-learning-enrollment-usa/.

Taleb 2020: Taleb, Nassim. *The Black Swan*. https://ig.ft.com/sites/business-book-award/books/2007/shortlist/the-black-swan-by-nassim-nicholas-taleb/.

The College Fix 2020: "This 'Genius' Professor's Higher Ed Tech Prediction Has College Leaders Worried." *The College Fix*, May 15, 2020. https://www.thecollegefix.com/bulletin-board/this-genius-professors-higher-ed-tech-prediction-has-college-leaders-worried/.

Tilman and Jacoby 2019: Tilman, Leo M., and Charles H. Jacoby. Agility: How to Navigate the Unknown and Seize Opportunity in a World of Disruption. Missionday, 2019.

Uhl-Bien, Marion, and McKelvey 2007: Uhl-Bien, Mary, Russ Marion, and Bill McKelvey. "Complexity Leadership Theory: Shifting Leadership from the Industrial Age to the Knowledge Era." *The Leadership*

Quarterly, Volume 18, Issue 4, August 2007, Pages 298–318. https://www.sciencedirect.com/science/article/pii/S1048984307000689.

Utz 2020: Utz, Richard. "Against Adminspeak." *The Chronicle of Higher Education*, June 24, 2020. https://www.chronicle.com/article/against-adminspeak.

Walsh 2020: Walsh, James. "The Coming Disruption to College: Scott Galloway Predicts a Handful of Elite Cyborg Universities Will Soon Monopolize Higher Education." *Intelligencer*, May 11, 2020. https://nymag.com/intelligencer/2020/05/scott-galloway-future-of-college.html.

Webb 2019: Webb, Amy. "How to Do Strategic Planning Like a Futurist." *Harvard Business Review*, July 20, 2019. https://hbr.org/2019/07/how-to-do-strategic-planning-like-a-futurist.

Wheatley 2006: Wheatley, Margaret. *Leadership and the New Science*. Berkeley: CA: Berrett-Koehler, 2006.

Wilden, Devinney, and Dowling 2016: Wilden, Ralf, Timothy Devinney, and Grahame Dowling. "The Architecture of Dynamic Capability Research Identifying the Building Blocks of a Configurational Approach." Academy of Management Annals, Volume 10, No. 1, January 1, 2016. https://journals.aom.org/doi/10.5465/19416520.2016.1161966.

Wilkinson and Kupers 2013: Wilkinson, Angela, and Roland Kupers. "Living in the Futures." *Harvard Business Review*, May 2013. https://hbr.org/2013/05/living-in-the-futures.

Wing 1988: Wing, R.L. *The Art of Strategy: A New Translation of Sun Tzu's Classic the Art of War*. New York: Main Street Books, 1988.

Yeo 2020: Yeo, Chuen. "Council Post: Why Agile Leaders Need to Be Master Strategists and Three Ways to Get Started." *Forbes*, June 8, 2020. https://www.forbes.com/sites/forbescoachescouncil/2020/06/08/why-agile-leaders-need-to-be-master-strategists-and-three-ways-to-get-started.

Yokoi 2020: Yokoi, Tomoko. "4 Agile Leadership Competencies to Outlast COVID-19." *Forbes*, June 2, 2020. https://www.forbes.com/sites/tomokoyokoi/2020/06/02/4-agile-leadership-competencies-to-outlast-covid-19.

A free ebook edition is available with the purchase of this book.

To claim your free ebook edition:

1. Visit MorganJamesBOGO.com
2. Sign your name CLEARLY in the space
3. Complete the form and submit a photo of the entire copyright page
4. You or your friend can download the ebook to your preferred device

Morgan James
BOGO™

A **FREE** ebook edition is available for you
or a friend with the purchase of this print book.

CLEARLY SIGN YOUR NAME ABOVE

Instructions to claim your free ebook edition:
1. Visit MorganJamesBOGO.com
2. Sign your name CLEARLY in the space above
3. Complete the form and submit a photo
   of this entire page
4. You or your friend can download the ebook
   to your preferred device

Print & Digital Together Forever.

Snap a photo

Free ebook

Read anywhere